PUERTO   DE   IBIZA

Obelisco a los Corsarios

vda.
Molina

Pl.
José Pidal

Andenes

LA   MARINA

S. Telmo

uz

Obispo Cardona

prim

Castela

Mayor

Virgen

Valencia

Retiro

Pl.
anal ejas Ant. Palau

Amadeo

Pedrera

aluarte S. Juan

Alfonso XII

Baluarte Sta. Lucia

Portal
de Tablas

Avd.

Gral. Franco

Pedro Tur

inario

n Román

Sta. María

Pl. España

Ayuntamiento

ALT VILA

po. Torres

Pl.
Catedral

P.º Episcopal

Catedral

PUNTA RATJADA

Bautista

Castillo

Baluarte S. Bernardo

Baluarte de S. Jorge

S'ARANY PETIT

FIGUERETAS

PUNTA MALLORCA

MOTONAVE A FORMENTERA
BUQUES CORREO A: PALMA
ALICANTE
VALENCIA
BARCELONA
MARSELLA

CARTOGRAFIA EVEREST

IBIZA

ESCALA GRAFICA

0   100   200

QUINTA EDICION

ISBN 84-241-4297-7
Depósito legal: LE-1434-1980
EVERGRAFICAS, S. A. - Carretera León-Coruña, km. 5 - LEON (España)

IBIZA
Y FORMENTERA

Text: FRANCISCO VERDERA RIBAS

Photography: J. Ciganovic
Oronoz
Zubillaga

Layout: Carlos J. Taranilla

AL MERITO TURISTICO

MINISTERIO DE INFORMACION
Y TURISMO — ESPAÑA

EDITORIAL EVEREST, S. A.

MADRID ● LEON ● SEVILLA ● GRANADA
VALENCIA ●ZARAGOZA ●BARCELONA ●BILBAO
LAS PALMAS DE GRAN CANARIA ● LA CORUÑA

A MADE-TO-MEASURE ISLAND

Ibiza —it has been written many a time— is an island made to man's measure, to the measure of the man attacked by the fatigue of haste. Nothing is colossal in Ibiza, neither distances nor proportions. Traffic lights, the few traffic lights controlling its brief haste, are a recent invention. All is within human distances. The island is not a racing world, but a pacifying one. It is not laziness, but peace, that keeps human positions there. A *livable* island. Never an earthquake. It does not snow (snow is a historical fact in the island). It rains just what is right, indispensable. The wind never attacks in fury. The sea is a homely sea. The sea is benignly blue. The sky is eternally blue. The round horizon is blue.

Ibiza, a minute island made larger by the tourist trade (and perhaps more uncomfortable and less intimate), is hardly 572 square kilometers in size, a great geographical brevity, but expanded and open in 170 kilometers of sea shore, useful all to the effects of tourist «exploitation» (it is preferable it were not so), perimeter that gives the exact measurement of its possibility and its shining touristic reality.

As large (or as small) as Corfu as Diodoro Sículo said, Ibiza belongs to the archipelago of the Balearic Islands, forming in turn, with Formentera and the islets of Espalmador, Tagomago, Conejera, Penjats, Vedrá, etc., the Pitiusas archipelago.

Ibiza is the third Balearic island in surface and in number of inhabitants, although, evidently, its personality even the historical one, is different from its two larger sister islands, Majorca and Minorca, to which it is united only by a very recent common history, many times merely administrative. For example, very few people from Ibiza have been to Minorca (and vice versa), an island which although loved, appears far and impossible...

Located to the west of Majorca, Ibiza is an island extraordinarily close to the two Mediterranean shores, only 52 miles from the Iberian Peninsula and 138 from Africa.

Panoramic view of the Ibizan coastline.

The Ibizan coast is made up of small coves.

One of the island's ports.

THE SUN AND THE BARBARIANS

The varied, the wide fortune of Ibiza is the sun. Ibiza, before Tourism, was already *inhabited* by the sun, by a product of the sun, salt, to which one arrives through its most absolute and purest action. Salt is the sun's great work, the sun in a great abundance, without intermediaries. Without salt, Ibiza, perhaps, would never have been inhabited until Tourism (as Enrique Fajarnés Cardona well says). The first settlers of Ibiza came to the island looking for salt. The first Ibiza industry was salt. Ibiza was Carthaginian thanks to salt. The first human call to Ibiza was brought by salt. Pure Tourism industry, Ibiza's newest mineral richness, the recent richness that multiplies its name, is also produced, almost minerally, by the sun, even if here there are more entrepeneurs, physical and chemical, of course.

In the first known description of the island, Diodoro Sículo's, which still may be in force, it is said that «it is cut by smiling fields and hills and it has a city called Ebusos and it is a Carthaginian colony», that «it also has ports worthy of mention and large walls and a number of admirably built houses» and that «it is inhabited by barbarians (foreigners) of all kinds...». It seems written today. Old are in the island, therefore, cosmopolitan lodgings, foreigners. Hence the total indifference of the Ibiza people (perhaps their most important vital attitude) to all that is alien. They are many centuries. Ibiza's national animal is the *ca eivissenc*, the famous Ibiza hound, wisely indifferent; a dog happy with a place in the sun, not necessarily comfortable; a whole beautiful Ibiza example. Dogs belonging to an enchorial breed maintained in its maximum purity in the island (as many other things) only identifiable in old Egyptian papyri. To the people of Ibiza also, who hardly open their wise and historical eyes as life goes by, the «bikini» is as good as the tunic, the barbarian is as good as the «hippy». They are many centuries.

Ibiza saltworks.

The typical Tablas Gateway and the «typical» hippies.

Formerly and today in the habitants of Ibiza.

A cave which was used as a dwelling by hippies.

In contrast, the island also offers other types of «accommodation».

CARTHAGE

Ibiza city, *Ebusos,* capital of the island, was founded by Carthage in 654 B., C. Carthage thus closed the way to the West (the always fabulous west) to the Greeks, their mercantile rivals, and ensured the old and strategic *way of the islands* (Sicile, Sardinia, Minorca, Majorca) that led to the route of the metals (copper in Huelva, silver that was Andalusian, tin from the Kassitérides islands, metal in which the Carthaginians had a profitable monopoly).

Ebusos was initially a colony of fishermen and fish salters. The salting industry was so important that Ibiza's products were exported to all Mediterranean countries, especially «garum», consisting in a visceral mixture of tune fish and cavalla, well appreciated by Greeks and Romans.

The Carthaginians of *Ebusos* were also good farmers. Dry figs, grain, onion, olives from Ebusos were famous in the old world (Pliny mentions Ibiza's figs with eulogy). Also famous was the rough Ibiza wine, still existing, whose roughness, apparently, was peculiar of Carthaginian wines.

They also elaborated purpura, at the cost of certain mollusks that were very abundant in the Ibiza coasts, purple murex *(múrex brandáris)*. And they transformed the lead of the island's mines in minium. The ceramics industries of Ebusos were especially important.

Ebusos became, with time, an important military base and an important factory, the third great Carthaginian establishment with the metropolis and Sardinia. Hence that the whole island is still a very rich archaeological field, more important, perhaps, than Carthage itself, destroyed by the Romans, and Sardinia, that soon underwent a total Romanization. The learned and studious, to reconstruct Punic culture and art, have to come to the island, having the second best museum in the World in this specialty, and where many lasting things still speak of Carthage.

Archaeological Museum. Punic mask.

Very old figure of a man.

Small statue of a woman.

SACRED SOIL

Pomponio Mela already indicated that Ibiza's soil had a prodigious condition refractory to all kinds of poison, a quality that still could be verified. since the island is entirely devoid of all kinds of poisonous animals and plants. From the toxicological innocuousness of the territory, it was easy to the people of old times to go to consider the island, in a firm belief, as sacred soil.

So, Ibiza became the island of Carthaginian sanctuaries. Ibiza was the island abundant in cemeteries, many of them (one went to die in the island). And due to the goodness of its clays, Ibiza's amphoras and Ibiza's terracottas were looked for and yearned for. (The same as today...)

It is well known that amphoras were then the universal container and that they were used for transporting or preserving cereals, wines, oils, salted products. The profusion with which they have been found in the old Ibiza sea, coming from very old shipwrecks, also indicates the great sea trade movement of the important Punic colony. All the Ibiza sea even today is a sea of amphoras.

Very abundant are also the terra cottas found, small figures in cooked clay representing divinities and sacred animals, of a rough and ineffable anatomy many a time, generally manufactured in series, and which were nothing but ex-votos offered to the many beneficial divinities, above all to goddess Tanit and god Bes, the highest gods of the island.

Tanit the Powerful had her temple in the Es Cuieram Cave, a grotto very near San Vicente cove, in the island's N.E., discovered in 1907, in which there was found a very interesting and small plaque, in bronze, offered —according to its text— «by Abdesmun, son of 'Azarba'al, the priest, for our Lady, for Tanit, the Powerful».

Bes, or Seventh Cabiro Eshmun, grotesque and intimate, a father god still dear to many Ibiza people, had his temple in Plana island, facing the present city of Ibiza.

Punic necklace made of vitreous paste and amulets. ▶

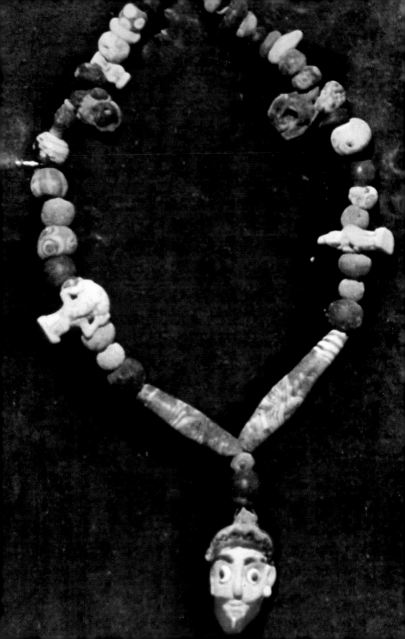

Sitting figure of the Goddess Tanit.

A bust of Tanit, an Ibizan Goddess.

NECROPOLIS

One went to Ibiza to die. Sacred soil. Soil to die on. Island-necropolis.

Punic people were characteristic for their deep love to the aged and forbears. Illustrious metropolitan old people were taken to Ibiza to die. Was there a better place? Illustrious metropolitan dead were taken to Ibiza to be buried in that soil that did not know of poison. (Mañá de Angulo believes in it, as otherwise, despite the news of the large population of *Ebusos* in its period of apogee, it would not be easy to explain the great abundance of burying-grounds, some very large, spread all around the island...)

The most important necropolis was that of *Puig des Molins,* very close to the present city of Ibiza, in which, according to some inventories, there are more than three thousand existing hypogeums, that sort of subterranean chambers dug in that limestone and funeral hill, whose use extended in the subsequent Roman domination of the island. This necropolis, declared a National Monument, is today, also, one of the great documents for studying Punic culture. The dead are resurrected. Many and very valuable objects have been exhumed and saved for authorized investigators and furtive ones, perhaps more numerous and avaricious, since the first archaeological excavations began there in 1903. There are numberless pieces having their origin there, today in the many museums, the many collections of all the world's antiquaries. And before that, through those swollen entrails, also crossed, implacable, the Arabian plunderers. What an amount of ill-fated funds!

In the sepulchral chambers of the hypogeums have been found amphoras, ceramics vases, jewels, amulets, vitreous paste necklace beads, seals in the form of scarabs, unguentaries, chandeliers, dressing table utensils (for example, razors), fishing utensils (hooks)... Signs of Punic life and Punic death. Extraordinary funeral garments.

Votive pitcher with Punic inscription.

Punic terracotta.

Hypogeum (Photo Archaeological Museum).

Polychromatic, Punic zoomorphic vessel from the necropolis at Puig des Molins.

Punic recipient similar to the previous one, also from the Puig des Molins necropolis.

ARCHAEOLOGICAL MUSEUMS

Ibiza city has two archaelogical museums, one in the *Puig des Molins* necropolis itself, monographic, containing the ruins found in the necropolis, and another one in *Dalt Vila,* facing the Cathedral, within the walled city enclosure, showing the stock found in the many fields in the island.

The *Puig des Molins* museum shows unique and beautiful versions of goddess Tanit (as good looking as the Ibiza girls) and an interesting full body feminine figure, as well as funeral masks, jewels, a very rich collection of vases with animal form (rams, doves, horses, etc.) and the china placed in the hypogeums by the families so they could serve the dead in their possible nutrition after death.

Singularly curious is the collection of decorated ostrich eggs (animal that does not exist in the island), which were used as sacred vases, The ostrich egg had the protoplasm, vital, that would brig the dead back to life...

Very important also is the series of coins shown, coined in Ibiza, with god Bes on one of the sides.

The *Dalt Vila* Archaeological Museum occupies one of the most noble of Ibiza's buildings, despite its outer humbleness and its precarious inside conditions, Ibiza city hall until 1838, when it was moved to and old Dominic order convent. The museum's building has three bodies, in three different styles: baroque, mudejar (it was built as a city hall after the Christian reconquest) and gothic (erected in the XIIIth or XIVth century by the Brotherhood of Sailors to install there a chapel dedicated to the Lord's Transfiguration).

The former Court.

A bust of the Carthaginian Goddess Tanit.

Face of a Punic idol. Detail.

CONFEDERATED CITY

Carthage beaten by Rome, Ibiza was not subjected by arms, rather it made a pact with Rome when its fealty to the vanquished metropolis had no purpose. A friendly pact, through which Rome granted Ibiza the condition of confederated city with full recognition of its autonomy and personality. Ibiza, thus, under Roman domination, continued to be fully Punic, and its structures and human systems changed very little. Ibiza continued to be a blooming naval and mercantile factory, exploited its salt beds and its lead mines, kept its fishing industries, elaborated purpura, exported amphoras and its agricultural products and minted its own money (the obverse has the head of emperors Augustus, Claudius and Caligula, the reverse the Cabiro Eshmun, which may give an idea of how Ibiza kept alive its Punic personality...).

Thus, Ibiza changed little with Rome. Romanization was slow, directly exerted. Ibiza had its same rights, the same liberties, exact beliefs and religious practices, the same own jurisdiction and was also free of serving in the legions, although it was bound to maintain auxiliary troops.

Rome took potable water to Ibiza city and ruins of existing aqueducts are still referred to by a chronicler of the XVIIIth century on the road from Ibiza to Las Salinas and in Santa Gertrudis and Santa Eulalia.

Three beuatifiul Roman statues are presently preserved in Ibiza, the three in the walled enclosure. Two, flanking its main door, the Portal de las Tablas (the Tablets Portal): one, a warrior (1.68 meters high), the other representing goddess Juno (1.55 meters), The third is a gowned aedile (1.92 meters), in the door of the Parade Quadrangle. The three statues are in marble, they are headless and were found in the Roman road of *Ses Figueretes* (also the present Vía Romana).

Ibiza lost its condition of confederated city in 70 A.D., when Vespasian granted the Latium law to all peoples of the Empire, an honor for all, though not for Ibiza, which was reduced to the condition of *municipium,* with the consequent taxes encumbrances, and lacking autonomy, although ruled by indigenous authorities.

The road up to Dalt Vila. ▶

The Tablas Gateway, one of the accesses to the walled city.

YEBISAH

With the end of the Roman domination begin five long centuries, hazardous and dark for the island, an island repeatedly assaulted and invaded, even if many of the successive episodes were little outstanding. In 425 it is the vandal king Gunderico who destroys the Balearic Islands, subsequently dominated by Genserico, and on 535 conquered by Belisario, who incorporates them to Byzantine Spain. In 711, the islands of Ibiza and Formentera go under Arabian power, succeeding in their possession the Caliphate of Córdoba, the emirs of Denia, the Almoravides, the Aben-Ganyas and the Almohades.

The Arabians again gave the old prosperity to the island, although with long and abundant intervals of blood and anguish.

Árabian chronicler Al-Makkari said that *Yebisah* (name the Arabians gave Ibiza) provided kindling wood and salt to a large part of Africa. «As in Yebisah —he added— there is a lot of forest, the main industry is making charcoal, shipped to Barcelona and other Mediterranean ports».

A great Arabian poet was from Ibiza, one of al-Andalus' best poets: Idris Ibn Al-yamani, also called Al-Sabini because of the many sabines existing in the island. «Heavy were —Al-Sabini wrote— the vases when they came to us empty, but when they were full of pure wine they got lighter and they practically flew with the content, the same way bodies are lightened by souls».

Physically, very few is left of the Arabian domination in the island: the network of canals created by them in *Ses Feixes*, in the vegetable garden zone that bordering the city, goes by the Ibiza-San Juan road; some ruin, in *Dalt Vila*, of the Arabian walls that also guarded Yebisah; some ceramics existing in the Archaeological Museum... The Arabian remained, however, indelible and contained in many Ibiza things: the words, the toponymy, the music, the usages, the indubitable race features and, also, in the indolence, frugality and little ambition of the people of Ibiza.

Ibizan countryside. View towards Cap Falcó and Formentera.

THE CONQUEST OF LANGUAGE

Jaime I of Aragón granted the conquest of Ibiza, as a feudal gift, to Guillermo de Mongrí, archbishop elect of Tarragona, who later was joined in the enterprise by infante Pedro de Portugal and Nuño Sans, count of the Rousillon. On 8 August 1235 Ibiza city was taken by the Catalonian conquerors. As tradition says, with some documentary base, the walled enclosure of Ibiza was taken tahnks to the treachery of the Moorish sheik's brother, in vengeance of the latter's taking his wife away, the cheated brother giving entrance to the conquering troops through a secret passage.

Since then, the popular language if Ibiza and Formentera, although not the culture, is the Catalonian (the eastern Catalonian, of Tarragona, Barcelona and Gerona), with notable particularities of a dilaect type, differentiating it not only from the continental language, but also —as indicated by Ibiza's poet Mariano Villangómez— from the subdialectal of Majorca and Minorca.

For historian Bartolomé Escandell Bonet the Catalonian conquest meant the island's Christian religious transformation and the entailment of the desired Ibiza products (especially salt and lumber) to the game of the Mediterranean economy of the crown of Aragón, while at the same time Ibiza came to enjoy also the western historical situation of that century.

Ibiza also since then was to be fully Hispanic.

Before the Christian conquest, the island was divided into five districts: Alhaueth, Xarch, Benizamid, Portumany and Algarb, named later by the conquerors Cuartón del Llano de la Villa, Santa Eulalia, Balanzat, Portmany and Las Salinas, respectively. The five quarters were reduced to four, two of them corresponding to Guillermo de Montgrí (who contributed double strength) and the remaining two to his conquest partners.

Detail of the Church of San Carlos; the limestone work is worth noting.

FIRST CONSTITUTION

Base and principle of insular law, per the consideration of Isidoro Macabich, the charter of franchises and liberties (of a great democratic spirit) that the conquerors generously granted the island's inhabitants is the authentic foundational constitution of the new insular life. A liberal constitution having nothing to do with the known feudal plan, which supposed the recognition of an important series of rights and privileges: exemption from duties, inviolacy of the home, intervention of Ibiza patriots in civil and criminal cases, etc.

The conquerors also recognize the participation of Ibiza inhabitants in profits from salt (participation that was later lost in the Succession war, when the profits from the salt beds were incorporated to royal income).

The organ of insular government was, for more than four centuries, the «University», in whose government bodies existed a just representation of all social estates. The «University» consisted of a Secret Council and a General Council. The Secret Council, in charge of ordinary matters, was formed by representatives of each of the three estates or «hands»: Big Hand (the gentlemen), Smaller Hand (sailors, merchants and craftsmen) and Foreign Hand (the peasants). The General Council handled the matters of greater importance and annual accounts were rendered to it.

Election of the councilmen was made by lots by means of bags for each estate («bag and lot system»).

Initially, the «University» met in the Major Church of Santa María, today Cathedral of Ibiza, from where it passed to the mudejar room of the present-day Archaeological Museum of *Dalt Vila*.

The Court of Arms in the walled city.

The Tablas Gateway with the Cathedral in the background.

Countrywomen in present-day.

An «adlib» shop.

THE CORSAIRS

The history of Ibiza is the history of landings, at least for four long centuries of fright and miseries. Ibiza, round and open to all seas and winds, was the object of constant pirate landings. The present tourist coast is not, naturally, the rough coast of the days of yore, in which all fear was possible. The sea was not our sea. Ibiza was too centrical for pirate days. Death or captivity was the frequent lot of Ibiza people and hence the growing insular depopulation. In 1392 the island's population was only 500 families. Formentera, in the xivth century, was totally depopulated.

If attack is the best defense, the island also had its corsairs who extended to the open seas the strict insular limits aboard their zebecs, fast sailing ships made from Ibiza pine trees by famous *mestres d'aixa* (shipwrights) in the island. There are one hundred seventeen glorious corsairs in Ibiza's annals with deeds that made history, from the xviith to the xixth century, the most popular figure being sailor Antonio Riquer Arabí, who on 1 June 1806, with his zebec «San Antonio y Santa Isabel», of 72 tons and two number eight guns, four number six and two number four, took by boarding, about five leagues to the south of the island, the British brig «Felicity», of 250 tons and twelve guns, under the command of Miguel Novelli, alias Papa de Ancona (Ancona's Pope), with home in Gibraltar for about thirteen years, also courageous and dreaded; he could not sign, because he did not know how, the proceedings instructed to search for the legitimacy of the prey. Five crewmen died in the «San Antonio y Santa Isabel», among them the own Ibiza corsair's father, 22 were wounded; eleven died and another 25 were severely wounded on board the «Felicity».

In the first centenary of the apprehension of the British brig, there was erected in the port of Ibiza an obelisk to its corsairs, the only monument in the world dedicated to remember corsairs.

The Ibiza sea is now in peace. It is everybody's sea.

The San Antonio coast with Cap Nonó behind.

Sundown on Conejera Island.

Sa Penya houses. In the background, the outline of the Cathedral.

FORTIFIED ISLAND

With all this, but with the Turkish pirate always lurking, it is not surprising that in an island repeatedly called to war, capital monuments are military: walls, lookout-towers and church-fortresses. (The man of Ibiza went to church to pray, but I suspect he went also to defend himself).

Ibiza was always a walled city. Prior to present day ones, there already existed a triple Arabian wall; and before these, the Carthaginian walls. Ibiza was creating its own island within the island.

Ibiza's present walls, perhaps the most important European fortress preserved intact, were built in thirty one years, a not-at-all disdainful record in view of the abundant stone making them strong brought by hired mules and peons. Thanks to the Turks, Ibiza, an island singularly forgotten by central power, has colossal walls to include now in the most typical tourist circuits.

Construction began by order of Carlos I, who entrusted the drawings to Italian engineer Juan Bautista Calvi, and was completed in 1585 under the reign of Felipe II. The cost of the work surpassed, three years before completion, 50,000 ducats, of which 20,000 Carlos I borrowed from the then archbishop of Valencia, Tomás de Villanueva, later a saint, who later condoned half of the royal debt.

Heptagonal in shape, seven are also the bastions of Ibiza's walls, which continue closing the oldest urban section.

There were fourteen strategically located lookout-towers that from the coast advised of non identified or enemy ships nearing the island. More humble monuments (as the humbleness of the island itself), but an eloquent testimony, even today, of those hazardous centuries. From these towers flew the smoke that warned the people of Ibiza of foreign danger and compelled them to the urgent need of putting out a face and protect women, children and old inside the walled temples of the island.

Monuments to old insular calamities.

Santa Eulalia. Puig de Missa church, in alt.

Ibiza. View of the walled city.

ADLIB

The island's peasants (almost unextant) had a beautiful own fashion of which practically nothing is left, except in professional festivals and other more or less folklore sprees. Only ten years ago it still was a majority. Today, only some old woman still wears the old Ibiza costumes, although, naturally, not in its glorious version. Five hundred, a thousand women must remain in the island still dressed in the old style, and all of them, unfortunately, nothing spright. The island began to lose its intact insularity with fashion. It has been the most spectacular historical assault suffered by the island and it has happened in the last twenty five years. The typical costumes are only used today, in a sort of photographic reserves nurtured by travel agencies, by organized folklore groups (which, on the other side, also accomplish a mission). But I expect that not many years will go by and the old Ibiza clothing will again be the gala costumes for at least those of us who still believe in their strange personality, originality and beauty. A model of a great Spanish fashion designer, inspired in the Ibiza costumes, was a sensation in the New York World Fair. A Spanish princess later was married in a beautiful dress of a total Ibiza inspiration. The old Ibiza models now inspire the creation of dressmakers located in the island, more than a hundred perhaps, of all races and nations, spread in unique «boutiques» who have consummated with a fabulous success the fortunate invention of a new Ibiza fashion, absolutely peculiar, the «adlib» fashion, *ad libitum* («dress as you like»), the fashion of liberty, the anti-fashion, a fashion half hippy, but, also, and mainly, half Ibiza's.

Ibiza has been for quite a few years, even before Carnaby Street, a certain and surprising capitality of young fashion. Ibiza again is an important fashion creating center.

A San Antonio street.

Shopping in the Ibiza streets.

Ibizan countrywoman. Facing the sea, her back turned on time.

THE «GONELLA»

The most beautiful typical Ibiza costume is the *gonella*, the oldest used by women, consisting in a tight black woolen tunic, pleated, reaching down to the feet; apron, also woolen, exquisitely embroidered; bodice with false sleeves and double row of gold or silver buttons. Over the shoulders, crossing over the bosom, an elegant shawl of furiously live colors, in silk (red, yellow). And on the head, the *cambuix*, a tight piece of stamped silk or a large white lace kerchief and, at times, a wide felt hat. For great festivals, they used the *mantellina*, white, an extraordinarily elegant piece. On the arm (almost a little as bull-fighters), the *abrigai*, a small garnet color cape. On their feet, pita sandals, espadrilles (the *espardenyes*), with esparto-grass soles, high and closed point. And jewels, the illustrious Ibiza jewels. The *emprendada*, in gold. Over the bosom, a silver and coral or mother-of-pearl necklace, and *sa joia* (the jewel) with images of saints on both faces, or a gold necklace, with rhomboid beads. Young girls engaged, with the fingers of both hands, except the thumbs, full of gold and silver rings from which hang a key and a heart. (Freud, if he had lived in Ibiza, could have explained, perhaps, the true phallic quality of this key, on the other hand so indispensable if the wedding, as usual, was with a maiden). The ahir-dress was very simple, the hair straight back, center parting and braided tail.

More modern than the *gonella* is the «white dress», in which the pleated tunic was substituted for a starched skirt, of lighter material, made round-looking thanks to several underskirts (underskirts that today can be «adlib» dresses). And on the head, a silk handkerchief, generally yellow.

But all of this begins to be a remembrance.

Girl in typical dress.

THE COCK

In winter, men wore black worsted trousers, pleated on the top, wide at the thighs and narrow in legs and ankles. In the summer, the trousers, made of cool linen, were white. At the waist, rolled, a red or black sash, fastened by sabine branch needle, sash in which the old-days men (only the old) kept a knife (knife which at times served not only for cutting bread), hero certainly of an exuberant red legend. Wide shirt, white, with high and starched collar. Black vest, in silk, with a double row of silver buttons. Silk kerchief at the neck. On the head a red cap with black cuffs, shorter than the Catalonian cap, or a palmetto leaves hat. On their feet, also pita *espardenyes,* with open point (diferential detail from the sandals used by women). (The materials were woven at home using linen, cotton and wool, all enchorial production).

So dressed, the Ibiza man, including his red crest, was a cock. He was also a cock when he danced, with his great possessive leaps drawing his territory. So similar to a cock of olden days, he always had a bizarre fame, and he also loved powder, perhaps an old Arabian reminiscence, perhaps a love acquired necessarily in this permanent land of frontiers the island always was, invaded and plundered by Algerian pirates (whose empire only ended in 1830), the Turkish ships, the Tunisian vessels, all so close, who had to be faced every day.

Since the reconquest of the island in 1235 through almost the second half of the xixth century, the Ibiza man lived permanently under arms, even in their own Militia, in which they were enlisted, all useful men, from the early age of sixteen until they were sixty.

Typical Ibizan dresses. ▶

Ibizan countrywomen in present-day wear.

An Ibizan rural dwelling.

An Ibizan dance.

POWDER

Blasco Ibáñez wrote that the pistol was the Ibiza man second language. A wild and elementary language. In effect, the Ibiza peasant even spoke of love with his gun or his pocket-pistol made by the insular blacksmiths themselves. Powder, thus, as a language and even as a compliment. For example, if the Ibiza man wished to allure the girl he loved, after mass he shot to the ground in front of her feet, and she had to show that she was not afraid at all. Also, when dances ended, the young blade could play homage to the loved one shooting at her feet. Disdain, on the contrary, was shown if the shot sounded at the girl's back. It was also seen as derogatory that peasant young men, on leaving the house where the *festeing* had been celebrated, shot their guns before the *bona nit* («good night»). The shot after the *bona nit* was a normal thing.

The pocket-pistols were also shot at the entrance and departure of processions from churches.

In the little squares in front of some country churches in the island (for example, San Miguel's) there is still kept *es mac de fer trons* («the thunder making stone»), a large stone embedded in the ground on which, during great festivals, the young men shot with their rifles and *trossos* (short and wide barrel rifles), moving spirally one after the other, doing what was called *es caragol* («the snail»). A wild and beautiful show, still remembered in the island.

Only a few years ago, on the eve of St. John the Baptist, which in the island is also the great fire festival, in many rural houses nine small bonfires were lit *(es nou foguerons)* which served as a target for the shots of relatives 'and neighbors' weapons.

Today there is in the island a growing fancy to skeet and squab shooting, sports more innocent than shooting at the Turk. But, of course, they are not new sports in the island...

Church of San Miguel.

THE «FESTEIG»

To it insular condition the island owes the maintaining, until a few years ago, of very old and peculiar usages, among them the *festeig* or courting, perhaps the best known, a whole beautiful and organized system of courting the young girl... Please consider that there were no meeting places for the young people of both sexes to establish their first acquaintances, in an island, in addition, in which the general dispersion of country dwellings (other small islands inside the island) made contacts difficult. Called by the *festeig*, a group of young men met, all over sixteen, to court the daughter or daughters of the family, after being authorized by the head of the family who received them. The *festeig* was held two or three times a week, in the evening. The young men arrived at the house, they in view of their number, agreed priorly on the time and on who sat first next to the *atllota* (girl). She came to the meeting, as is human wearing her best, and sat at a distance from the group of young men, who, meanwhile, except the one talking, made talk with the rest of the family. The young men, one by one, by strict turns and distributing the time justly, sat on the chair placed by the girl's side. If any of them exceeded the time, the next one warned him throwing a small stone at him. If he still exceeded the time, despite the warning, the fact was considered a dare and almost always there followed, outside the house, the fight. The future mother-in-law, all this time, in accordance with her secular calling, did not miss a detail and, inside, perhaps feeling young again, also had to select a son-inlaw... One by one, and in order to get to know each other better, as in today's dances (when the music does not deafen), although those acquaintances did not have to mean by force arriving to the last and formal consequences. The young blades courted here today and there tomorrow (like flying pollen). The girl was pleasant with all. There was no formal commitment in the *festeig*. Until a couple agreed. The engaged girl then appeared in public (high mass on Sunday) with her fingers full of rings with a key and a heart in chains.

Today, perhaps, the *festeig* would be the way around...

THE DANCES

A primitive dance, truly, the Ibiza dance, supreme archaic testimony of Spanish folk dance, kept in all its most absolute purity. One of the oldest of Spanish dances and one of the simplest. Perhaps the most naked dance. Vital dance: wild and powerful in the man, manly, arrogant, cock (let us say it once again) in his spectacular leaps; tame and sweet, perhaps surrendered, eyes low, the woman. A dance of pursue.

The man asks the woman to come out to dance with a husky and strong castanet blow (which, to me, deep inside, is only a sort of cock's crow).

The dance has two succeeding times: the *curta* and the *llarga*. In the *curta*, more quiet, the woman describes small circles in the figure of an eight (8), sliding softly, while the man follows her with small leaps, always looking at her.

The dance gains rhythm, livelier, in the *llarga*. The circles the woman describes are now wider. The man's leaps are more vigorous. The woman seems to get away from him, as if she wished to give him her back. The man, his leaps accompanied by strong castanet blows, looks for her face. The man, at the end of the dance, in a gesture of possession and kindness, passes his arms above her head and the young man bends, before her, his knee on the ground.

In the *dotze rodades* dance, nuptial in nature, only the bride and groom dance, extending with the *filera* dance, in which the bride is accompanied by another two damsels, the three facing the groom, although it was evident that his preference was for his bride, as he steadily looked at her (at least, officially).

In nuptial festivities, the *curta* was generally started by parents and grandparents, the bride and groom following later, they went around three times and retired, and then the guests get in the dance, which they follow with the *llarga*, after which came the *dotze rodades* and the *filera* dance.

Dances which still are a surprise for folklore students. Dances that have obtained many extraordinary prizes in international festivals and the most prestiged national festivals.

Musicians of the San José ballet. ▶

Typical dances.

MUSIC AND SONGS

Ibiza's musical intruments, also enchorial and the purest craft-manship production, accompanying dances and songs, are the *flaüta* (made of oleander wood, with metallic inlayings), the *tambor* (beautifully and ingenuously decorated), the *castanyoles* (large cas-tanets made of common juniper, about 15 centimeters long) and the *espasí* (a steel rapier, used only to accompany the *caramelles*, Christmas carols sung during Christmas Eve mass). The *flaüta* —as has been indicated by García Matos— is a real *beak* flute with a made mouthpiece and three finger holes, made on the bottom end of the tube. Its scale is diatonic. The player accompanies himself with the *tambor*, a small tambourine that hangs from his left arm, with which and he also holds the *flaüta*, which he hits with a wooden small club grabbed in his right hand. The music is generally im-promptu, enchorial, naturally. None of the players know music.

Sheepherds (are there any left in the island?), for solace, use (or used) the *reclam de xeremies*, a double reed clarinet, home-made also, similar to the maït of old Egypt (as noted by García Matos) and the zoummârah of the present-day shepherds of Low Egypt.

In the songs, *cantades* or *xacotes*, in response to an archaic musical style whose enigmatic origin it has not yet been possible to find, although Isidoro Macabich (the great Ibiza intellectual figure) deems a deeply marked Arabian influence in it, particularly in the peasant song with ruffles, the singer (or female singer) is only accompanied by the *tambor*, marking the rhythm with slow hits. The lyrics, in the Ibiza language, are usually delicious. Its authors, generally illiterate, did great efforts to memorize them. In the *porfedi* (strife) songs, in which the ample popular ingenuity intervenes, they succeeded each other with impromptu lyrics of a burlesque type about love and its participants, a man and a woman. This real contest of sharpness and malice —as Juan Castelló very well said— was (is) simply delicious.

Musicians of the San Miguel ballet.

THE ARCHITECTURE

Probably the most original thing in Ibiza, this island full of original things, is its architecture, studied and copiously reproduced in new times, in the bungalows filling the long Mediterranean coasts. Many «VIPS» even have their Ibiza style bungalow in the shining Côte d'Azur. Ibiza architecture doubtlessly has a name and a prestige since its absolute relationship was found with modern functional architecture, and since its many and wily inventions were discovered. The first one, its austerity, purifying all kinds of useless forms and spaces. The Ibiza house is humble, simple, livable. The second one, its funcionality. The house grows as family needs grow. The primitive nucleus is seen added to new cubes with a new specific application: *sa casa de geure* («The house to sleep in»), *sa casa des carro* («The cart's house»), *sa casa des gra* («the grain's house»), etc. The third one, the surprising and intuitive beauty of the groups so created. The coomon room is the *porxo*, entry room, where, at the sun's strongest hours, rests are very refreshing. When he is not working out, the Ibiza peasant spends his hours there. A room for life in common: there the visits, the *festeig*, the living room, the dining room. There is always a calendar with the Sacred Heart of Jesús, family photos, military photos, First Communion photos, the sewing macbine, the Ibiza chairs with the braided esparto-grass seats, the long and narrow table (latter and former of a very beautiful design), *es banc gerré* (for the eater jugs), *es tinell* (cornice where the bread is kept).

Inside and out, lime, the lime of centuries, lime over lime, that gives the walls Tapies' beautiful qualities. (Lime, «so early, so manual; so invasive!», Enrique Fajarnés Cardona has written). «White Island» Ibiza was called by Santiago Rusiñol, a name that today, who would have said it, is its geotouristic denomination.

A typical house of the island.

The Ibizan rural dwellings are small and combine so well the geometry of their form with Nature itself.

The new buildings, constructed for tourists, are inspired by the lines of old Ibizan architecture.

CINDERELLA

The *Espòlits,* the most fundamental of Ibiza's juridical institutions, very frequent among peasants, are the marriage articles agreed and set up —as written by Ibiza's jurist José Costa Ramón— by the contracting parties prior to marriage, which include: gifts by reason of marriage, that the wedding couple's parents give their children reserving the life usufruct of the gift; the bride's dowry; the community property; and the *heredamiento* (tenement). The separate property system rules in the island. As regards community property, absolute separation also rules, except that otherwise is agreed in the *Espòlits,* in which case the most frequent formula is dividing the patrimony in a proportion unequal for the husband (one fourth for the wife and three fourths for the husband). Regarding the *heredamiento ibicenco* (Ibiza tenement), last contract included by the *Espòlits,* it consists in the gift the marrying couple makes of their present and future property on behalf of the unborn children, that morally ties the family property to male sons (generally preferred to female), although said gift does not comport any limitation to the full and absolute ownership on the part of the donors. The *heredamiento ibicenco* institution tries to avoid as much as possible property division. The *hereu* (the heir), the eldest male son, gets the largest and best part, while the others have to take the legitime. This supposed that the optimum and profitable lands were always for the *hereu,* while the others, who usually received the poor quality lands, had to emigrate to América or Algiers, become priests or enter from the ground floor in a military career. But, suddenly, Tourism modifies all the structures and those second class lands are in most cases the coastline lands and pine tree forests desired by development and hotel promoters, the millionaire lands. Again, the story of Cinderella in Ibiza. The *hereus* continue tilling their fields. The disinherited of yore, not any more. At heart, this kind of vengeance of a legal type has not been unjust...

Another example of an Ibizan house.

OTHER RURAL CUSTOMS

The *estatge*, another common law institution peculiar to Ibiza's peasants, is —according to jurist José Sáez Martínez— the special right of use and lodging conferred by parents to chidren who remain unmarried or exceptionally disabled for work, which was not limited to the right of getting a lodging, but was accompanied by the assignment of certain uses and services, such as use of the oven, kitchen and well, as well as the right to eat fresh fruit. The *estatge* was the grant of an independent home for those whom, due to the strict tenement rule, could be threatened of being excluded from the soil they were born in.

Another curious custom of a legal nature in Ibiza is the right of way known as *caminos de ir a misa* (the road to mass), frequently named in public documents. The *caminos de ir a misa* are lanes linking one or several granges with the parish church or the public way leading to it whose purpose is facilitating religious services (burials, weddings, viaticums, baptisms, masses, etc.). An owner, for example, having in his farm a *camino de ir a misa* can not eliminate it at his will, or vary or restrict it.

The *aparcería* —studied by jurist José Costa Ramón— is the agricultural contract most frequent in the island. Generally it is executed verbally and practically never in writing, beginning and ending on the festivity of St. John the Baptist (24th of June), date on which the farming year ends and begins. The share-cropper, called *majoral*, receives one half of all the products of the farm, has free housing and uses for his support various products of the operation, being bound to cultivate the land with his own animals and furnish the agricultural tools and carts necessary for the operation. L'amo (the owner) and the *majoral* share half and half the payment of taxes, seed, chemical fertilizers and manure. The owner is in charge of planting trees, repairs and improvements and the purchase of props for trees. The crop obtained is divided in two while the owner is present, the *majoral* doing the cut and the owner the choice.

Church of San Carlos.

Typical Ibizan windmill.

The Cathedral and Dalt Vila from the San Juan highway.

*The white town
houses of Ibiza climb
up to Dalt Vila.*

Sa Penya.

Olive-trees on the island.

THE ISLAND

The island surprises with the dispersion of its white granges. The island, the whole island, is a white architectural splash. It is the sole perpetual insular snow. Small white islands within the island. Except for three important urban nuclei, the Ibiza people always fled wisely from human crowds, perhaps, initially, by the fright of foreign invasions. With dispersion, naval artillery lost its efficiency. Dispersion, on the other hand, required from the enemy coming by sea larger territorial displays. Even today the population lives dispersed. The municipal and human nucleus, the *parroquia* (parish), is reduced to the church, some store-bars (selling the thousand and one items necessary for the frugal peasant life), some houses and the school. The neighbors around go to the *parroquia* to mass or their purchases, almost exclusively.

Another surprising thing in the island is the saints' toponymy. All the island's towns have saints' names, of those to whose appellation the church that centered, capitalized and defended the neighborhood has been dedicated.

But the island of Ibiza is, fundamentally, the sea. The sea is the great Ibiza reference. All landscapes lead to the sea. The sea is always present and live, as witness or hero, in any insular landscape.

And its Mediterraneancy. Ibiza is a Mediterranean island one hundred per cent. It is in its grasses, its trees, its pine forests, its sabine trees. Almond, fig, olive, carob trees have an extensive abode in Ibiza. And pine, populating profusely the abundant mountainous profiles. Pine served the Greeks to name the island.

An island rich in water, the nice green of its fields is surprising, fields today abandoned many of them because Ibiza's peasants think more promising the tourist crop... Where lettuce and cabbage grew years ago suddenly may rise a white and flamboyant development in Ibiza.

A locust-tree, common in Ibiza.

Panoramic view of Ibiza seen from the Cathedral.

Ibizan handicraf

THE ISLAND'S CAPITAL

Ibiza, the island's capital, is a city climbing up a mountain, high, upped, vertical, sky scraping, finished up high by its Cathedral, the old acropolis. City with more than twenty seven centuries of history.

Two are the fundamental urban Ibizas: the one included inside the walled enclosure, the oldest, the foundational, and the one spreading out outside the walls, port city, seafaring city, mercantile city.

Ibiza was granted the title of city by a Royal Charter of the 22nd of October of 1783.

Dalt Vila and *Sa Penya* district have been declared a «monumental historical group». *Dalt Vila* is the walled Ibiza.

Ibiza begins in the sea, in its port. The port, in islands, is the plural eating mouth through which enter in the insular digestion the overseas products and with them, also, news (another indispensable insular merchandise) until in 1860 Ibiza established telegraphic communication with the Continent and with Majorca.

Even today, in the port, no longer the peaceful port of years ago, one can see the Ibiza sailing vessels, successors of the famous zebecs, to which present-day urgencies have changed the sails for the engine.

From the sea, to the left, the *Sa Penya* district, with an extraordinary architectural enchantment, port and Mediterranean district, which today Ibiza fishermen share with «boutiques», the most famous «hippy» bars and the studios and ateliers of artists and writers. White and labyrinthic district, which by force one has to roam through.

To the right, also from the sea, *La Marina* and the impersonal and inevitable modern districts in which it is repeatedly proven that present-day Ibiza people build living spaces worse than our ancestors.

Urban venter is the Vara de Rey promenade, whith a monument dedicated to this Ibiza general, hero of the Cuban war.

Further, again with a sea will, the districts of *Figueretas, Es Vivé* and *Den Bossa* beach.

Partial view of the port of Ibiza.

Sa Penya with the Cathedral in the background.

The arrival of another boat at the port of Ibiza.

Another view of the port.

A Sa Penya street.

Sa Penya goes down to the edge of the sea.

A Sa Penya «cosmopolitan» street.

A view of Vara de Rey Walk.

Vara de Rey Walk.

The Cathedral, the Church of Santo Domingo and Sa Carrossa.

An Ibizan street.

The beach at Figueretas and the tourist complex which has grown up around it.

DALT VILA

All *Dalt Vila,* the old matrix district, opens up on lookouts
to the sea. There is a lot to look at from *Dalt Vila.* From the lookout
on plaza de España, to the right, in the background, Formentera
island. From the lookout on the Cathedral square, down below,
Ibiza's bay and the port, and the island, a great part of the island,
expanding, green and with vegetation, to the horizon. A district to
look at and see. Because there is a lot to see, also, in *Dalt Vila.*

The Cathedral, Gothic, erected by the Christian conquerors and
reconstructed not too fortunately in the xviiith century and later
pillaged in 1936. Of the primitive building only the belfry tower
remains, necessary in the unmistakable silhouette of Ibiza. In the
Cathedral are kept an interesting custody of the xivth century, a
beautiful Renaissance relief of Our Lady of the Rosary and Gothic
tablets of Santiago and St. Mathew.

On the Cathedral square are also located, the Archaeological
Museum of *Dalt Vila,* the Curia (with a beautiful Gothic door)
and the Castle, already mentioned by Tito Livio and, later, in 1403,
by Ruy González de Clavijo, a military building that today is a
sumation of architectural styles, having an interesting medieval
tower. And on the same square, the episcopal palace, humble and
austere, residence of the bishops of the Ebusos' see. (Ibiza already
had its own bishop in 484, Opilio. In 1782 Pope Pius VI made Ibiza
a bishopry.)

Casa Laudes (Laudes Manor), one of the noblest of Ibiza's
buildings, belonging to Catalonian Gothic, today the see of the
Instituto de Estudios Ibicencos (Institute of Ibiza Studies).

The Dominic order convent, built in 1591, today occupied by the
City Hall, and Santo Domingo church, baroque, end of the xvith
century, in which a fire in 1971 destroyed valuable frescoes in its
dome.

The Museum of Contemporaneous Art, in the old Officers Hall
of the Ibiza Royal Force, with background of works rewarded in
the Ibiza Biennial International Art shows and the work of the
best of Spanish present young artists and many and important
foreign painters living in the island.

Ibiza is a favourite haunt of artists.

Bastion of the Portal Nou.

A street in Ibiza.

The Cathedral from the Church of Santo Domingo.

Another view of the Cathedral with its unmistakeable bell tower.

Ibiza City-Hall.

SAN JOSE

The modern insular airport is located in the municipal district of San José, on the island's S. W. *Es Codolar*, one of the millionaire national airports, also near San José are the so old Ebusos salt beds.

The Ibiza salt beds occupy a surface of about 400 hectares, from 0 to 0.70 meters below sea level. There are forty pools in which salt is formed from day to day. The salt beds are located in a zone in which the mean yearly evaporation is 1,200 liters per square meter. Annual salt production is over one hundred thousand tons, most of it exported to European northern countries. *Las Salinas*, has the only railroad in the island, a dear, little, almost funny little train. In the small *Las Salinas* port, *La Canal*, where ships sailing under all flags operate, the Ibiza people learned to speak English before tourisn was invented. In 1871 the salt beds were sold by the State (a very poor business deal) to a private company for 1,160,000 pesetas.

The Ibiza people, who enjoyed the community property of the income from salt, when they wished to remit a debt or needed to make some saving, went to *Las Salinas* to work, a tough and parching job, work of implacable task days, today softened by machines. The salt man was a courageous man.

San Francisco de Paula, the salt beds parish church, the humblest in the island, does not have a burial ground. It is the only one in the island that does not have one. The brackish soil of the zone would eternally preserve the corpses in brine.

On the road from Ibiza to *Las Salinas*-Airport is San Jorge, whose xivth century church should be visited.

Next to the urban nucleus of San José (also with an interesting xviiith century church) is located the highest peak in the island, *Sa Talaia*, 475 meters high, and *Ses Roques Altes*, 345 meters, sadly famous for a very serious airplane accident that happened there.

Many beaches in the San José municipal district, apart from those located in San Antonio bay: *Cala Conta, Cala Tarida, Cala Vedella, Cala D'Hort*, etc.

The Church of San Jorge. ▶

San Francisco de Paula in Las Salinas.

Interior of the Church of San José.

Tarida Cove in San José.

One of the island's sunny beaches.

Sunset over the sea.

The Ibiza coast.

Detail of San Antonio bay.

Cala Bassa with the Cap Nonó behind.

SAN ANTONIO

To the island's west is San Antonio, the old Portus Magnus of the Romans, big port, big bay, privileged tourist zone of the island, perhaps the most international, perhaps the noisiest, where especially a youth tourist trade has a date.

All San Antonio is hotel or apartment or is on the way to be. As Fajarnés Cardona has well written, if in old days the fortress was the island's largest construction, today it is the hotel.

The urban nucleus, always exuberant with life, multicolor, populated perhaps by the best looking tourist women in Europe, is an unforgettable spectacle.

The bay is closed, shared by San Antonio on the south with the municipality of San José, by Conejera island, about three kilometers long, uninhabited, famous because it was said that the great Carthaginian chief Hannibal was born there. The bay has several beaches: *Cala Bassa, Port des Torrent, Playa Pinet, Es Puet, Ses Sevines, Cala Gració.*

San Antonio's church, the other great local monument, after the bay and its irreproachable blue sea, was built in the XIVth century.

San Antonio, which was a small fishermen town, now has a beautiful seaside promenade leading to the new port, in which yachts of all flags arrive.

In the San Antonio municipal district are located, about two kilometers from the city, the ruins of Santa Inés catacombs church, as well as, also in a precarious state, *Ses Fontanelles* cave, located near cape Nonó, with interesting rupestrian paintings attributed to the Bronze Age.

From San Antonio a wonderful tour can be made by sea to Vedrá islet, S. W. of the island, a wild rock, 388 meters high only inhabited by wild goats.

The bay of San Antonio.

Two views of San Antonio Promenade.

Church of San Antonio.

A view of San Antonio port.

Church of San Rafael.

The beach at Po.: des Torrent.

*The little island
of Es Vedrá rises
out of the
blue sea.*

SANTA EULALIA DEL RIO

Santa Eulalia del Río, town located in the eastern coast of the island, has always lived a little with its back to the sea. Its town life had elapsed parallel to the sea, perhaps because Santa Eulalia is the core of the island's richest and most fertile region. Santa Eulalia was the island's vegetable garden. But now Santa Eulalia also looks toward the sea and tourism, the newest Ibiza manna.

Santa Eulalia has the only river in the Balearic islands, running about eleven kilometers, certainly not very abundant in water.

Santa Eulalia's church, built in 1568 and located atop a small hill, *Es Puig de Missa*, is one of the island's most beautiful temples and an example, illustrious, of its church-fortresses. In *Es Puig de Missa* exists a beautiful and unique grouping if Ibiza constructions, in which the «Barrau Museum» is located in one; this museum is anthological of this Catalonian painter, who did his most important work in Santa Eulalia.

On the square in front of the City Hall a monolith reminds of the humanitarian action of Santa Eulalia inhabitants in rescuing the crew and passengers of the S. S. «Mallorca» shipwrecked in its coasts in 1913.

Santa Eulalia's municipal district has important tourist nuclei: those on *Es Canar* and *Calallonga* beaches and those on *Siesta*, *S'Argamassa* and *Roca Llisa* (which has an excellent golf course).

Santa Eulalia has always had an excellent gastronomical tradition. Its restaurants have always had a great prestige in the island.

Very interesting are the visits to the parishes in this municipal district: Jesús and San Carlos, the first with a xivth century church, which has an exceptional retable attributed to Rodrigo de Osona; and San Carlos, with the old lead mines.

Cala Llonga, a tourist zone. ▶

The Puig de Missa fortified church of Santa Eulalia.

View of the beach at Cala Llonga.

Es Canar beach.

◀ *A magnificent view of Den Bossa beach.*

The Santa Eulalia coastline.

Es Canar beach.

Portinatx beach.

Porch of the church of San Miguel.

San Miguel with the church above.

SAN JUAN BAUTISTA

The municipal district of San Juan Bautista groups four small urban nuclei: the parishes of San Juan, San Miguel, San Lorenzo and San Vicente Ferrer, all with very beautiful and humble churches according to Ibiza's architectural models, especially San Miguel, perhaps the most beautiful church in Ibiza, a fortified church also built on a small hill, called also, as Santa Eulalia del Río's, *Puig de Missa*.

San Lorenzo has one of the most unique architectural groups in the island: old town of Balafi, a dwelling group that arose with a primarily defense purpose under cover of two fortified towers in which, in danger, the families in the neighborhood made a stronghold. The neighbors went up the towers thanks to step-ladders that they later removed.

San Juan, capital of the region, is one of the island's most intact towns. The landscape is still the old landscape, almost the original one. It seems the typical mountain town (of the relative island mountains), rather Pyrenean (of the relative island's Pyrenees). Perhaps the most intact Ibiza people, in this Ibiza time of universalization and unification, also grow there.

From San Juan, inland town, one goes through different roads to two of the island's best beaches: Cala Portinatx and Cala San Vicente, whose wild beauty has not yet been surrendered. When king Alfonso XIII landed in Cala Portinatx in 1929, during some naval maneuvers, people began calling the beach Portinatx del Rey.

Bordering Cala San Vicente is Tagomago islet, uninhabited, where perhpas the most savory of black groupers of the Ibiza seas are caught. Next to Cala San Vicente is Es Cuieram cave, the old Tanit temple.

The Balanzat port beach is also very pretty, in San Miguel, and the rough coast above a splendidly blue sea in Na Xamena.

Gothic altarpiece in the church of Nuestra Señora de Jesús.

Cala Bassa, Ibiza.

Panoramic view of Es Canar.

Another fine view of Es Canar.

Cala Xarraca.

Port de Saint-Michel.

The rugged coastline of Na Xamena.

Various islets with Formentera in the background.

FORMENTERA

Formentera's horizont, physical and human, is Ibiza, island from which it is, from coast to coast, only three miles, and eleven, from port to port.

Formentera is the fourth island in surface (115 km²), and population. With Ibiza it comprises the Pitiuso Archipelago, piny, thus called by the Greeks due to the great profusion of pine trees in its hills. Formentera, small and cereal island was the old Frumentaria (wheaty island) of the Romans.

Ibiza and Formentera practically have the same history. Almost total is the human identity, the usages, the modes and mores. From Ibiza, or descendants of Ibiza people are Formentera's present inhabitants, an uninhabited island where they settled.

Flat island, its maximum height is 192 meters, on the south of it, *La Mola*. The island has a 37 mile perimeter.

Es Pujols beach.

The Freos strait separates Formentera from Ibiza. Between the two larger islands are the islets *Es Penjats* («The Hangers»), *Pou, Espalmador* (with perhaps the most beautiful Mediterranean beaches, ar at least the most solitary and Robinsonian), *Espardell* and *Espardelló*.

Formentera is an absolute island. Insularity is lived totally and implacably there. The maximum distance in the island is 14 kilometers, on its widest part, from East to West.

There are four towns in Formentera: San Francisco Javier (the capital), La Sabina (the island's port) and San Fernando and El Pilar.

Formentera is also a salt island. The salt beds are important, with yields even larger than those in Ibiza.

Perhaps the most notable geographical accident in old Frumentaria are the two large pools, in the north of the island, used through history as fish nurseries: *Estany des Peix* («fish pond») and *Estany Pudent* («ill-smelling pond»). The first is used today for water ski.

Formentera saltworks.

AN UNHURRIED ISLAND

Old ruins belonging to the Bronze Age found in Formentera refer the establishment of an old and initial township. However, for many centuries the historical constant in Formentera has been the lack of population. Life was difficult in *Frumentaria*, through centuries easy prey of pirates and even their refuge.

In 1246 Guillermo de Montgrí cedes Formentera in feud to Berenguer Renart for him to resettle.

In its large periods of depopulation, Formentera, however, was used for agriculture by the Ibiza people. Its fields were planted and cattle was raised there.

In 1726 San Francisco Javier church was built, particularly curious because it was armed, The Formentera man also was a man in constant war. The Formentera Urban Militia distinguished themselves in the xviiith century with their special bravery in the almost constant strife against the pirates decimating the island.

In 1807 a group of Spanish and French astronomers established in Formentera one of the vertices for measuring the meridian passing through Dunquerque, Paris and Formentera.

Formentera has been the last great tourist discovery of latter years. It has exceptional beaches, as *Es Pujols* and *Migjorn*, with calm and transparent waters.

Archduke Luis Salvador of Austria, who visited the islands very much in 1866 and 1888, noted the estraordinary old age of the people of Formentera, the highest in the country, apparently. Formentera is an unhurried island.

The Ibiza-Formentera sea trip, with modern launches, is a delicious picnic, very recommendable. The tour or the trip to Formentera is a must.

One of the small boats which make the crossing to Formentera.

Es Caló beach.

INFORMACIÓN PRÁCTICA IBIZA
INFORMATION PRATIQUE IBIZA
PRACTICAL INFORMATION IBIZA
PRAKTISCHE HINWELSE IBIZA

Para cualquier otra información, puede Vd. dirigirse a la Oficina de Turismo de Ibiza, sita en: Vara de Rey, 13.

Pour toute information, vous pouvez vous adresser au Bureau du Tourisme de Ibiza, situé: Vara de Rey, 13.

For further information, visit the Tourist Office in Ibiza, located at: Vara de Rey, 13.

Zur Erhaltung irgendeiner anderen Auskunft können Sie sich an das Tourismusbüro dieser Ortschaft in der Ibiza: Vara de Rey, 13.

a isla de Ibiza, situada en el mar Mediterráneo, es la tercera en extensión y la más occidental del archipiélago balear, con una superficie de 572 km² y unos 40 000 habitantes. Muy próxima a las dos orillas mediterráneas, Ibiza dista tan solo 52 millas de la Península Ibérica y 138 de África. Descubierta para el comercio por los fenicios, desfilaron por Ibiza los pueblos más característicos de la antigüedad. Su capital, llamada también Ibiza, fue fundada por los cartagineses 654 años antes de Jesucristo. Los cartagineses dieron a la isla el nombre de «Ibosim» y los romanos «Ebusus». Los árabes la llamaron «Yebisah». En el año 1235 la reconquistó, en nombre de la Corona de Aragón, don Guillermo de Montgrí.

El aspecto de la ciudad de Ibiza es tan singular como pintoresco. Una acrópolis dominada por una Catedral y rodeada de pequeñas casas cúbicas, de blancura deslumbrante bajo un cielo azul turquesa. La arquitectura ibicenca, con su espiritual y maravilloso primitivismo, sobre todo en el ambiente rural, constituye una fuente de inspiración de artistas y arquitectos.

Impresionantes murallas rodean la ciudad. Fueron construidas por el ingeniero romano Calvi en 1554, por orden del emperador Carlos V.

De relieve accidentado, la isla ofrece paisaje de incomparable belleza. En el suelo ibicenco se suceden, en una hermosa policromía, el bosque de pinos (Ibiza fue llamada Pitiusa, pinosa, por los griegos) y los almendros tan característicos. Hay higueras y olivos. También hay palmeras, que reconocen la proximidad biológica de África y el soplo de su viento. Y existe la noria árabe, y el molino de viento, que, en Ibiza, reemplazan casi por entero a la nube y a la lluvia.

'ile d'Ibiza, située en mer Méditerranée, la plus occidentale de l'archipel baléare, a une population de 40 000 habitants. En ce qui concerne sa superficie elle vient au troisième rang, avec 572 km². Elle est très près des deux rivages méditerranéens et n'est située qu'à 52 milles de la Péninsule Ibérique et 138 de l'Afrique. Découverte pour le commerce par les Phéniciens, les peupls les plus caractéristiques de l'antiquité y défilèrent. Son chef-lieu, appelé également Ibiza, fut fondé par les Carthaginois en l'an 645 av. J.C. Ils lui donnèrent le nom d'«Ibosim» et ensuite les Romains «Ebusus». Les Arabes, eux, l'appelèrent «Yebisah». Au nom de la Couronne d'Aragon, elle fut reconquise en 1235 par Guillermo de Montgrí.

L'aspect de la ville d'Ibiza est aussi original que pittoresque. Une acropole est dominée par une Cathédrale et entourée par de petites maisons cubiques, dont la blancheur est aveuglante sous un ciel bleu turquoise. L'architecture d'Ibiza, avec ce côté primitif à la fois spirituel et merveilleux, surtout en dehors de la ville, constitue une source d'inspiration pour les artistes et les architectes.

De magnifiques remparts entourent la ville. Ils furent construits en 1554 par l'ingénieur Calvi, sur ordre de l'Empereur Charles V. De relief accidenté, l'île offre un paysage d'une incomparable beauté. Sur le sol d'Ibiza se succèdent, dans une belle polychromie, le bois de pins (Ibiza fut appelée Pitiusa par les grecs, où les pins sont abondants) et les amandiers si caractéristiques. Il y a des figuiers et des oliviers. Il y a aussi des palmiers qui rappellent la proximité biologique de l'Afrique et l'influence de ses vents chauds. Ile existe la noria arabe et le moulin à vent, qui, à Ibiza remplacent presque entièrement le nuage et la pluie.

The island of Ibiza, located in the Mediterranean sea, is the third largest and the western-most of the Balearic archipelago, with a surface of 572 km² '343.2 m) and about 40 000 inhabitants. Very close to the two Mediterranean shores, Ibiza is only 52 miles from the Peninsula and 138 from Africa.

Discovered for commerce by the Phoenicians, the most characteristic peoples of old times went through Ibiza. Its capital, also called Ibiza, was founded by the Carthagenians 654 years B.C. The Carthagenians named the island «Ibosim» and «Ebusus» the Romans. Arabians called it «Yebisah». In 1235 it was reconquered, in the name of the crown of Aragón, by D. Guillermo de Montgrí.

The aspect of Ibiza city is as unique as it is picturesque. An acropolis dominated by a Cathedral surrounded by small cubic houses, with a blinding whiteness under a turqueoise blue sky. Ibiza's architecture, with its spiritual and marvelous primitivism, above all in the rural ambient, is a source and fountain of inspiration for artists and architects.

Impressive walls surround the city. They were built by engineer Calvi in 1554, under orders of Emperor Charles V.

Of a hilly nature, the island offers scenery of unequalled beauty. On Ibiza soil a succession of pine-woods (Ibiza was called by the Greeks Pitiusa —piny—) and the characteristic almond-trees produce a beautiful polichromy. There are fig and olive-trees. There are also palm-trees that recognize the biological proximity of Africa and the blowing of its wind. The Arab chain pump and windmill still exist, chich in Ibiza replace, almost completely, the cloud and the rain.

Die insel Ibiza, im Mittelmeer gelegen, ist die

drittgrösste Insel in Bezug auf die Ausdehnung und die westlichste Insel der Balearen. Sie hat eine Oberfläche von 572 km² und etwa 40 000 Einwohner. Ibiza liegt in der Nähe der beiden Mittelmeerküsten, von der Iberischen Halbinsel beträgt die Entfernung nur 52 Meilen unter einem Afrika 138 Meilen.
Sie wurde für den Handel von den Phöniziern entdeckt und die bekanntesten Völker der Antique zogen durch Ibiza. Die Hauptstadt heisst auch Ibiza. Sie wurde 654 vor Christus von den Karthagern gegrundet. Diese gaben der Insel den Namen «Ibosim», und die Römer nannten sie «Ebusus», die Araber «Yebisah». Im Jahre 1235 wurde die Insel im Namen der Krone von Aragonien durch Guillermo de Montgrí zurückerobert.
Der Anblick der Stadt Ibiza ist ebenso eigenartig wie malerisch. Eine Akropolis, beherrscht von einer Kathedrale und umgeben von kleinen kubischen Häusern in einem blendenden Weiss unter einem türkisblauen Himmel. Die Architektur von Ibiza mit ihrem wunderbaren geistigen Primitivismus, besonders in ländlichen Gegenden, ist eine Quelle der Inspiration für Künstler und Architekten.
Eindrucksvolle Mauern umgeben die Stadt. Sie wurden von dem römischen Ingenieur Calvi im Jahre 1554 auf Befehl des Kaisers Karl V. gebaut.
Die leicht hügelige Insel erfreut sich einmalig schöner Landschaftsstriche. Pinienhaine (die Griechen nannten die Insel Pitiusa, d. h. reich an Pinien) wechseln mit den so charakteristischen Mandelbäumen ab. Es gibt Felgen- und Olivenbäume, sowie Palmen, die auf die Nähe Afrikas und seine warmen Winde hinweisen. Auch das arabische Schöpfrad und die Windmühlen, die auf Ibiza fast ganz Wolken und Regen ersetzen, fehlen nicht.

Formentera

La isla de Formentera, la cuarta del archipiélago balear por su extensión —unos 115 km² y unos 3 500 habitantes—, está situada al sur de Ibiza, de la que está separada por el paso de «Es Freus», y de cuya capital, desde el puerto de La Sabina, en Formentera, dista solamente once millas.
El paisaje es extremadamente bello y variado, si se tiene en cuenta la topografía y extensión de la isla. Se compone de dos cabos muy elevados, el de Berbería, al sur, y el de La Mola, al este, ambos son de una agreste belleza, con espesa pinada y descienden sobre el mar, formando abruptos acantilados. El centro de la isla se extiende en una larga y estrecha depresión que termina al norte con dos grandes estanques y

unas salinas. Todo el litoral está bordeado d hermosas playas de blanca arena.

L'île de Formentera, la quatrième de l'archipe baléare avec 115 km² et environ 3.500 habi tants, est située au sud d'Ibiza, dont elle es séparée par le passage de «Es Freus». D port de la Sabina à Formentera, on est seu lement à 11 milles du chef-lieu.
Le paysage est extrêmement beau et varié, s l'on tient compte de la topographie de l'île e de son extension. Elle comprend deux cap très élevés, celui de Berbería, au sud, et celu de la Mola, à l'est. Les deux sont d'une grande beauté agreste, avec une pinède dense et face à la mer elles forment des fa laises abruptes. Le centre de l'île s'étend e une longue et étroite dépression qui finit a nord par deux grands étangs et des salines Tout le littoral est bordé de magnifiques plage au sable blanc.

Formentera island, the fourth largest of the Ba learic archipelago in extension —about 11 km², and 3 500 inhabitants, is locate in the southern part of Ibiza, from which is separated by the «Es Freus» pass, an from whose capital, from the La Sabina por in Formentera, there are only eleven miles The landscape is extremely beautiful and va ried, if one takes into account the topo graphy and the extension of the island. It composed of two very high capes, Berbería to the South, and La Mola to the East, bot have a rough beauty, with dense pine grove going down to the sea, forming abrupt cliffs The center of the island extends in a lon and narrow depression ending on the Nort with two large pools and salt beds. Th whole sea coast is full of beautiful white san beaches.

Die Insel Formentera ist die viertgrösste Inse der Balearen mit einer Ausdehnung von etw 115 km und 3 500 Einwohnern. Sie liegt s dlich von Ibiza und ist durch eine Meerenge die «Es Freus» von ihr getrennt. Zischen d Hauptstadt Ibiza und dem Hafen La Sabin auf Formentera liegen nur 11 Meilen. D Landschaft ist ausserordentlich schön un verschiedenartig, wenn man die Topograph und die Ausdehnung der Insel in Betrac zieht. Sie besteht aus zwei sehr erhöhte Caps, das der Berbería im Süden und das de Mola im Osten. Beide sind von wild Schönheit mit dichten Pinienhainen und la fen im Meer aus, wo sie scharfe Steilküste bilden. Die Mitte der Insel breitet sich auf e ner langen und schmalen Senke aus, welch im Norden mit zwei grossen Teichen und e nigen Salinen endet. Die gesamte Küste e tlang ziehen sich herrliche Strände mit wei sem Sand.

ARTE Y CULTURA
ART ET CULTURE
ART AND CULTURE
KUNST UND KULTUR

1.1. CONJUNTO MONUMENTAL
ENSEMBLE MONUMENTAL
MONUMENTS
SEHENSWÜRDIGKEITEN

LA MARINA
LA MARINA
LA MARINA
LA MARINA

Es uno de los barrios que más llama la atención del visitante, especialmente si su llegada es por mar. Se extiende a lo largo de los andenes del muelle, formando ciudad y puerto un solo cuerpo. Las edificaciones responden al módulo clásico ibicenco. Los cafés y bares montan sus terrazas junto a los muelles, entremezclándose entre ellas velas y redes, estibas de carga y mástiles de veleros. Este conjunto forma de por sí uno de los más bellos atractivos de la ciudad.

C'est l'un des quartiers qui frappe le plus le visiteur, surtout s'il arrive par mer. Il s'étend sur tous les quais, la ville et le port ne faisant qu'un. Les constructions correspondent au module classique d'Ibiza. Les cafés et les bars ont leurs terrasses à côté des quais, s'y mêlant voiles et filets, arrimages et mâts de voiliers. Cet ensemble constitue l'une des merveilles de la ville.

This is one of the districts claiming the greatest attention of the visitor, especially if he arrives by sea. It runs along the dock's platforms, city and port forming one sole unit. The buildings are of the classical Ibiza module. The cafés and bars open their terraces next to the docks, in an intermingling of sails and fishing nets, load bins and sail-boat masts. This aggregate is in itself one of the most beautiful attractions of the city.

Dies ist eines der Stadtviertel, auf welches der Besucher besonders aufmerksam wird, vor allem wenn er vom Meer her nach Ibiza kommt. Es zieht sich dem Hafendamm entlang, so dass die Stadt und der Hafen eine Einheit bilden. Der Baustil entspricht der klassischen Bauart Ibizas. Die Terrassen der Cafés und Bars reichen bis zu den Molen, wo Segel, Netze, gestaute Lasten und Masten von Segelbooten bund durcheinander liegen. Dieser Stadtteil ist von ganz besonderer Anziehungskraft.

OBELISCO A LOS CORSARIOS
OBELISQUE AUX CORSAIRES
OBELISK TO THE CORSAIRS
OBELISK DER KORSAREN

Se levanta en los andenes del muelle, junto al arranque del malecón central. Los ibicencos lo erigieron en recuerdo de sus heroicos corsarios, los cuales alcanzaron su máximo relieve en el siglo XVIII y comienzos del XIX, frente a la piratería morisca y a las marinas en guerra contra España.

Il s'élève sur le quai, à côté du départ de la jetée centrale. Les habitants d'Ibiza le construisirent en souvenir de leurs héroïques corsaires dont la gloire culmina au 18e et début du 19e ss, face à la piraterie mauresque et d'autres flottes en guerre contre l'Espagne.

It is erected on the dock's platforms, next to the starting point of the center dock. The people of Ibiza erected it to remember the heroic corsairs, who reached their maximum glory in the XVIIIth century and early in the XIXth, against Moorish pirates and the navies in war against Spain.

Er befindet sich am Hafendamm neben dem Beginn der mittleren Mole. Die Einwohner von Ibiza haben ihn zum Gedenken der heroischen Korsaren errichtet, die ihren grössten Erfolg im XVIII Jahrhunderts und Anfang des XIX. Jahrhunderts gegen die maurische Piraterie und die mit Spanien im Krieg befindlichen Seemächte verzeichneten.

BARRIO DE LA PEÑA
QUARTIER DE LA PEÑA
LA PEÑA DISTRICT
BARRIO DE LA PEÑA

Este barrio es quizá el más característico de la ciudad de Ibiza. Está formado por un intrincado laberinto de pasadizos y estrechas callejuelas, situado a caballo entre el muelle y el antiguo baluarte de Santa Lucía en forma ascendente. Forman sus calles y escaleras un conjunto único. Pese a su angostura, no hay oscuridad. La blancura deslumbrante de sus casas reverbera durante el día, bajo el intenso sol, y por la noche brillan, plateadas, bajo la luna. Su población está constituida por pescadores y marineros. Su pintoresquismo ha sido fuente de inspiración de numerosos artistas.

C'est probablement le plus caractéristique de la ville d'Ibiza. Il est formé par un labyrinthe inextricable de passages et d'étroites ruelles et se situe à cheval entre le quai et l'ancien donjon de Santa Lucía. Ses escaliers et ses rues sont absolument uniques. Bien que ce soit excessivement étroit, le quartier n'est pas pour autant dans l'obscurité. La blancheur éblouissante de ses maisons luit pendant tout le jour sous le soleil intense, et, pendant la nuit, elles brillent, et sont toutes d'argent, sous la Lune. C'est là que vivent les marins et les pecheurs. Son aspect pittoresque a inspiré maint artistes.

This is perhaps the most characteristic district of Ibiza city. It is formed by an intricate labyrinth of alleys and narrow streets, straddling the dock and the old Santa Lucía bulwark in an ascending manner. Its streets and stairs form a unique whole. Despite the narrowness there is no darkness. The blinding whiteness of the houses blazes in the day-time under the intense sun, and at night they shine, silvery under the moonlight. Its population is fishermen and sailors. Its picturesquism has been the fountain of inspiration of many artists.

Dies ist vielleicht das bezeichnendste Stadtviertel von Ibiza. Es ist gebildet aus einem verworrenen Labyrinth von Gängen und schmalen Strässchen, und liegt zwischen der Hafenmole und der alten Bastion Santa Lucía bergaufwarts. Seine Strassen und Treppen bilden eine einmalige Gesamtheit. Trotz seiner Enge ist es nicht dunkel. Das blendende Weiss seiner Häuser strahlt tagsüber unter der brenneden Sonne und nachts leuchten die Häuser silbern beim Mondschein. Die Bewohner sind Fischer und Seefeute. Dieses malerische Bild hat vielen Künstlern Inspiration zu ihrer Aarbeit gegeben.

RECINTO AMURALLADO
LES REMPARTS
WALLED ENCLOSURE
DIE MAUERN

Esta fortificación es la única en su género que se conserva intacta en Europa. Su conjunto ofrece la figura de un heptágono irregular, del cual se destacan siete baluartes. Tiene tres puertas de acceso. Fueron construidas, sobre las antiguas murallas edificadas por los árabes, por el emperador Carlos V en 1554 y según planos del ingeniero Juan Bautista Calvi. Su testimonio más completo en Europa del arte militar del siglo XVI, y están declaradas Monumento Nacional.

Cette fortification est l'unique en son genre qui reste intacte en Europe. Elle a la forme d'un heptagone irrégulier, d'où se détachent sept donjons. Il a trois portes d'accès. Elles furent contruites, par ordre de Charles-Quint en 1554 d'après les plans de l'ingénieur Juan Bautista Calvi, sur les anciens ramparts edifiés par les Arabes. C'est le témoignage le plus complet en Europe de l'art militaire du

XVIème siècle. Il est déclaré Monument National.

This fortress is the only one of its type kept intact in Europe. It has the figure of an irregular heptagon, out of which seven bulwarks stand out. It has three access doors. They were built, over the old walls erected by the Arabs, by Emperor Charles V in 1554 in accordance with drawings made by engineer Juan Bautista Calvi. They are the most complete witness of European military art of the XVIth century and they have been declared a National Monument.

Diese Befestigungsmauern sind die einzigen ihrer Art, die in Europa unzerstört erhalben blieben. Im Gesamten bilden sie ein unregelmässiges Siebeneck mit sieben hervortretenden Bastionen. Es gibt drei Zugangstore. Diese Befestigung wurde durch den Kaiser Karl V. im Jahre 1554 nach Plänen des Baumeisters Johann d.T. Calvi auf den alten, von den Arabern errichteten Mauern erbaut. In Europe sind diese Mauer der beste Zeuge der militärischen Kunst des XVI. Jahrhunderts. Sie sind National denkmal.

PORTAL DE LAS TABLAS
PORTAL DE LAS TABLAS
PORTAL DE LAS TABLAS
PORTAL DE LAS TABLAS

Es la entrada principal al recinto amurallado. El origen de su nombre arranca de su antiguo puente levadizo, que se proyecta ahora reconstruir. La corona, un gran blasón de los Austrias, con una leyenda en latín, recordando que en 1585, bajo el reinado de Felipe II, fueron terminadas estas murallas. La flanquean dos estatuas romanas.

C'est l'entrée principale de l'enceinte. Le nom vient de l'ancien pont-levis que l'on pense reconstruire aujourd'hui. Elle est couronnée par un grand blason des absbourg, comportant une légende en latin rappelant que c'est en 1585, sous le règne de Philippe II, que furent terminés ces remparts. De chaque côté, se trouvent ces statues romaines.

This is the main entrance to the walled enclosure. The origin of the name comes from its old draw-bridge, today planned of being rebuilt. The crown, a great coat of arms of the House of Austria, with were completed in 1585 under the reign of Philip II. It is flanked by two Roman statues.

Dies ist der Haupteingang zum ummauerten Bezirk. Der Name hat seinen Ursprung von der alten Zugbrücke her, deren Rekonstruktion geplant ist. Uber dem Portal ist eine grosse Wappentafel der Osterreicher mit eine lateinischen Inschrift, die daran erinnert, dass 1585, unter der Herrschaft von Philipp II diere Mauern vollendet wurden. Zu beiden Seiten befinden sich zwei römische Statuen.

D'ALT VILA
D'ALT VILA
D'ALT VILA
D'ALT VILA

Se llama así en ibicenco la parte de la ciudad enclavada intramuros, siendo, por tanto, quizá la más interesante y de más sabor local; aquí hallaremos, entre un sinfín de construcciones de máximo tipismo, las antiguas casas señoriales, el Ayuntamiento, con su bellísimo mirador sobre el mar, la antigua iglesia de Santo Domingo, el Museo Arqueológico y la Catedral.

C'est ainsi que l'on appelle la partie de la ville située derrière les murs, et présente un grand intéret et une grande saveur locale; là, on trouve, parmi les nombreuses constructions très typiques, les vieilles maisons seigneuriales, la Mairie, avec son magnifique panorama sur la mer, l'église ancienne de Santo Domingo, le Musée Archéologique et la Cathédrale.

This is the name, in the Ibiza language, of the city located inside the walls, being, therefore, the most interesting, with the most local touch; here we find amidst numerous constructions of the maximum typism, the old manor houses, the City Hall, with its beautiful look-out to the sea, the old Church of Santo Domingo, the Archaeological Museum and the Cathedral.

So wird in der ibizenkischen Sprache der Stadtteil genannt, der innerhalb der Mauern liegt. Daher ist dieses Viertel vielleicht das interessanteste und das typischste; hier finden wir eine Unzahl gan typischer Bauten, die alten Herrenhäuser, das Rathaus mit seiner wunderbaren Aussicht auf das Meer, die alte Kirche Santo Domingo, das Archäologische Museum und die Kathedrale.

IGLESIA DE SANTO DOMINGO
ÉGLISE DE SANTO DOMINGO
CHURCH OF SANTO DOMINGO
KIRCHE SANTO DOMINGO

Comenzó su construcción a fines del siglo XVI y es la iglesia del antiguo convento de San Vicente Ferrer, de la Orden de Santo Domingo. Bello retablo de la capilla de Nuestra Señora del Rosario, de sencillo barroquismo. Reviste también interés su bóveda, al fresco, y los azulejos que decoran los basamentos.

Le début de sa construction date de la fin du XVIe siècle; c'est l'église de l'ancien couvent de San Vicente Ferrer, de l'ordre de Saint-

Dominique. Beau rétable de la chapelle de Notre Dame du Rosaire, de style baroque simple. Sa voute revet un grand intéret, ainsi que la fresque et la faïence qui décore les soubassements.

Its construction began toward the end of the XVIth century and it is the church of the old monastery of San Vicente Ferrer, or the Dominique Order. A beautiful retable in the chapel of Our Lady of the Rosary, simply baroque. Also interesting is its vault, with fresco paintings and the tiles decorating the bases of the columns.

Der Bau wurde Ende des XVI. Jahrhunderts begonnen. Sie ist die Kirche des alten Klosters San Vicente Ferrer, des Dominikanerordens. Es gibt ein schönes Altarbild in der Kapelle Nuestra Sra. del Rosario in einfachem Barockstil. Auch die Kuppel mit Freskenmalerei ist interessant, ebenso wie die Kacheln, die den Fussboden zieren.

LA CATEDRAL. *LA CATHÉDRALE*
THE CATHEDRAL. *DIE KATHEDRALE*

Fue erigida por acuerdos de los conquistadores de la isla, en los siglos XIII y XIV, y en el mismo solar que en otro tiempo se alzaron los templos romanos y musulmanes. Lamentablemente, la reconstrucción de que fue objeto a mediados del siglo XVII no resultó muy feliz, resintiéndose en ello su puro gótico inicial. Es digna de admirar su bellísima Custodia, de plata dorada con preciosos esmaltes, del siglo XIV. Es curioso que, siendo el clima de la isla tan bondadoso y los fríos prácticamente desconocidos, la catedral haya sido puesta bajo la advocación de Nuestra Señora de las Nieves.

Elle fut construite sur décision des conquérants de l'île aux XIII et XIVe siècle à l'endroit même où se trouvaient jadis les temples romains et musulmans. Malheureusement, la reconstruction dont elle fut l'objet (vers le milieu du XVII) ne fut pas particulièrement heureuse, nous faisant regretter le gothique pur initial. Ne manquons pas d'admirer son magnifique Ostensoir, en argent doré avec de très beaux émaux, du XIVe siècle. Il est curieux que malgré le climat doux de l'île où les froids rigoureux sont inconnus, la cathédrale ait été mise sous le vocable de Notre-Dame des Neiges.

It was built by agreement of the conquerors of the island, between the XIIIth and the XIVth centuries, on the same site of the old Roman temples and Moslem temples. Unfortunately the reconstruction it was subjected to in middle XVIIth century was not too good a one, its pure Gothic initial style suffering with it. Worthy of admiration is its very beautiful Custodia, made of gilt silver with precious enamels, of the XIVth century. It is a curious fact that the island having such a benign climate in which cold is practically unknown, the cathedral is placed under the advocation of Our Lady of Snows.

Sie wurde auf Beschluss der Eroberer der Insel im XIII. und XIV. Jahrhundert errichtet, und zwar auf dem gleichen Grundstück, wo früher die römischen und muselmanischen Tempel standen. Leider war der Wiederaufbau Mitte des XVII. Jahrhunderts nicht sehr glücklich, so dass die anfängliche reine Gotik darunter zu leiden hatte. Besonders bewundernswert ist die sehr schöne Monstranz aus vergoldetem Silber und Email aus dem XIV. Jahrhundert. Es ist seltsam, dass die Kathedrale trotz des milden Klimas der Insel, auf der die Kälte fast unbekannt ist, der Sra. de las Nieves (der Jungfrau des Schnees) gewidmet ist.

IGLESIA DE JESÚS
ÉGLISE DE JÉSUS
CHURCH OF JESÚS
JESUSKIRCHE

Del siglo XV, reedificada en el XVI. Con pintoresco pórtico. El retablo de su altar es una joya pictórica de la primitiva escuela valenciana.

Du XVe siècle, réédifiée au XVIe siècle, avec de pittoresques portiques. Le retable de son autel est un joyau pictural de l'école primitive de Valence.

Belonging to the XV Century, was rebuilt in the XVI Century. With a picturesque portico. The altar-piece is a pictorial masterpiece of the Valencian school.

Aus dem XV. Jahrhundert, im XVI. wiedererbaut. Mit einem malerischen Säulengang. Das Altargemälde ist ein Juwel der primitiven valencianischen Schule.

PORTAL NOU. *PORTAL NOU*
PORTAL NOU. *PORTAL NOU*

Es uno de los tres accesos del recinto amurallado, situado a Poniente; siendo, por tanto, nuestra salida obligada para dirigirnos al «Puig des Molins».

C'est l'un des trois accès des remparts, situé à l'est. Nous devons, par conséquent, passer par là pour arriver au «Puig des Molins».

It is one of three accesses to the walled enclosure, located toward the West, being, therefore, our compulsory outlet to go to the «Puig des Molins».

Es ist einer der Zugänge zu den Mauern, der im Westen liegt. Wir müssen durch dieses Tor, um zum «Puig des Molins» zu gelangen.

PUIG DES MOLINS. *PUIG DES MOLINS*
PUIG DES MOLINS. *PUIG DES MOLINS*

Saliendo de intramuros por el Portal Nou, se levanta frente a nosotros la fina silueta de la colina denominada «Puig des Molins». Aquí se encuentra la antigua necrópolis púnica que data del siglo VII antes de Jesucristo, con prolongación en la época romana. A su lado se ha construido un museo monográfico del más grande interés. Existen en ella más de 4 000 hipogeos abiertos en la roca, y su estudio ha atraído la atención de los más famosos arqueólogos.

En sortant de l'encceinte par le Portalotas devant nous s'élève la colline appelée «Puig des Molins». C'est là que se trouve l'ancienne nécropole punique qui date du VIIe siècle av. J.C. allant jusqu'à l'époque romaine. Juste à ses côtés, il y a un musée monographique qui revet un grand intéret. On peut voir plus de 4 000 hypogées ouvertes dans le rocher. Leur étude a attiré de célèbres archéologues.

Leaving the walled enclosure through Portal Nou, we find in front of us the fine silhouette of the hill called «Puig des Molins». Here we find the old Punic burial grounds, dating back to the VIIth century B.C., with extended use in the Roman period. Beside it has been built a monographic museum of the greatest interest. There are in it more than 4,000 hypogea opened in the rock, and its study has drawn the attention of the most famed archaeologists.

Wenn wir durch das Portal Nou aus dem Bezirk innerhalb der Mauern herauskommen, erhebt sich vor uns die feine Silhouette des sogenannten «Puig dels Molins»-Hügels. Hier befindet sich die alte punische Totenstadt aus dem VII. Jahrhundert v. Chr. bis zur römischen Epoche. Daneben wurde ein monographisches Museum von grösstem Interesse gebaut. In der Totenstadt öffnen sich im Felsen 4.000 Grabstätten, deren Studium die berühmtesten Archäologen aufmerksam gemacht hat.

VARA DE REY. *VARA DE REY*
VARA DE REY. *VARA DE REY*

Encontramos este paseo a la entrada de Ibiza de regreso a la ciudad. Se llama así en memoria del general ibicenco Vara de Rey (1840-1898), que murió gloriosamente en la defensa de El Caney (Cuba). En el centro de este señorial paseo se alza un bello monumento en su honor, inaugurado en 1904 por el Rey don Alfonso XIII. Contribuyó, paradójicamente, a la suscripción abierta para erigirlo, el antiguo rebelde cubano Quintín Banderas.

Cette promenade est située à l'entrée d'Ibiza lorsque l'on revient vers la ville. Elle porte ce nom en mémoire du général d'Ibiza Vara de Rey (1840-1898), qui mourut glorieusement en défendant El Caney (Cuba). Au milieu de cette grandiose promenade, se dresse un magnifique monument en son honneur. Il fut inauguré en 1904 par le Roi Alphonse XIII. Aussi paradoxalement que cela puisse paraître, l'ancien rebelle cubain Quintín Banderas contribua à la souscription ouverte pour l'ériger.

We find this promanade as we enter Ibiza on returning to the city. It gets its name from commemorating Ibiza's general Vara de Rey (1840-1898), who died gloriously in the defense of El Caney (Cuba). In the center of this seignorial promenade is a beautiful monument in his memory, inaugurated in 1904 by King Alfonso XIII. As a paradox, to the subscription opened for its erection contributed the old Cuban rebel Quintín Banderas.

Wir stossen auf diesen Paseo auf unserem Rückweg am Eingang der Stadt Ibiza. Dieser Paseo trägt den Namen zum Gedenken des ibizenkischen Generals Vara de Rey (1840-1898), welcher glorreich bei der Verteidigung von El Caney (Kuba) ums Leben kam. In der Mitte dieses herrschatlichen Paseos befindet sich das zu seinen Ehren gebaute schöne Denkmal, welches im Jahre 1904 von König Alfons XIII. eingeweiht wurde. Paradoxerweise trug der alte Rebell aus Kuba Quintín Banderas bu der Suskription für den Aufbau bei.

1.2. MUSEOS
MUSÉES
MUSEUMS
MUSEUM

MUSEO ARQUEOLÓGICO
MUSÉE ARCHÉOLOGIQUE
ARCHAEOLOGICAL MUSEUM
ARCHÄOLOGISCHES MUSEUM

Se trata de uno de los museos más importantes en arte púnico. La mayoría de los objetos que atesora proceden de las excavaciones realizadas en «Illa Plana» y la cueva de «Es Cuieram». Es visita obligada para todo viajero, e incluso los indiferentes quedan im-

presionadísimos a la vista de los valores que encierra.

Il s'agit d'un des musées les plus importants de l'art punique. La plupart des objets qu'il renferme proviennent des fouilles réalisées à «Illa Plana» et de la grotte de «Es Cuieram». Chaque visiteur se fait un devoir de s'y rendre; en effet, meme les indifférents ne restent pas insensibles à la vue des richesses qui y sont exposées.

This is one of the most important Punic art museums. The majority of the objects treasured come from excavations made in «Illa Plana» and the «Es Cuieram» cave. Its visit is a «must» for all travelers, and even the indifferent are impressed in view of the valuables in it.

Es handelt sich um eines der bedeutendsten Museen punischer Kunst. Die Mehzahl der dort befindlichen Gegenstäude stammen von Ausgrabungen, welche in «Illa Plana» und der Höhle von «Es Cuieram» vorgenommen wurden. Diesen Besuch sollte jeder Reisende machen, selbst die Gleichgütigen werden sehr beeindruckt sein, wenn sie die Schätze sehen, welche dieses Museum enthält.

MUSEO DE ARTE CONTEMPORÁNEO
MUSÉE D'ART CONTEMPORAIN
CONTEMPORARY ART MUSEUM
MUSEUM FÜR MODERNE KUNST

Contiene numerosas colecciones de pinturas y esculturas de arte contemporáneo.

Contient de nombreuses collections de peinture et de sculpture d'art contemporain.

Contains numerous collections of paintings and sculptures of contemporary art.

Es enthält eine stattliche Sammlung zeitgenössischer Gemälde und Skulpturen.

MUSEO DE LA CATEDRAL
MUSÉE DE LA CATHÉDRALE
CATHEDRAL MUSEUM
KATHEDRALE-MUSEUM

Su primera sala fue sede de la Universidad (Consejo de cien miembros que regía el municipio de Ibiza y Formentera); la segunda fue capilla de El Salvador, del gremio de marineros. Su contenido es de carácter general, destacando los hallazgos del santuario de Tanit, de la isla Plana y del Puig d'en Valls.

Sa première salle fut le siège de l'Université (Conseil de cent membres qui gouvernait la municipalité d'Ibiza et de Formentera); la deuxième salle fut la Chapelle du Sauveur, de la corporation des marins. Son contenu est de caractère général où l'on remarque les découvertes du Sanctuaire de Tanit, de l'île Plana et du Puig d'en Valls.

Its first was the seat of the university (a Council of one hundred members that governed the municipality of Ibiza and Formentera); the second was the Chapel of «El Salvador» belonging to the sailors association. Its contents are of a general character, most remarkable of which are, the findings from the Sanctuary of Tanit, Plana island and Puig d'en Valls.

Der erste Saal war früher Sitz der Universität (Rat der hundert Mitglieder, die das Munizipium Ibiza und Formentera regierten); der zweite war die Kapelle des Hl. Erlösers vom Marinegremium. Der Inhalt ist allgemeiner Art, wobei besonders die Fundstücke aus dem Heiligtum Tanit, der Insel Plana und Puig d'en Valls hervorzuheben sind.

MUSEO ÉTNICO
MUSÉE ETHNIQUE
ETHNIC MUSEUM
ETHNISCHES MUSEUM

Interesante colección de objetos relacionados con la vida primitiva.

Intéressante collection d'objets racontant la vie primitive.

Interesting collection of objects related whit primitive life.

Interessante Sämmelstücke über das primitive Leben.

NECRÓPOLIS PÚNICA. Puig des Molins.
MUSEO TAURINO DE LA PLAZA DE TOROS.

1.3. BIBLIOTECAS
BIBLIOTHÈQUES
LIBRARIES
BIBLIOTHEKEN

CAJA DE PENSIONES. Vía Púnica, 2.
INSTITUTO NACIONAL DE ENSEÑANZA MEDIA. Ignacio Wallis, s/n.
SEMINARIO CONCILIAR. Juan Ramón, 2.

1.4. ARTESANÍA
ARTISANAT
GRAFTWORK
KUNSTHANDWERK

ARTESANÍA IBICENCA. Alfarería. Exhibiciones de torno. Aragón, s/n.

2. ALOJAMIENTOS
LOGEMENTS
ACCOMODATION
UNTERKUNFTE

2.1. HOTELES
HÔTELS
HOTELS
HOTELS

Ibiza

ARGOS. Playa de Talamanca. H***.
CARABELA. Playa d'en Bossa, s/n. H***.
GOLETA. Playa d'en Bossa, s/n. H***.
IBIZA-PLAYA. Playa Figueretas, s/n. H***.
SIMBAD. Playa Ses Figueres. H***.
CENIT. Archiduque Luis Salvador, s/n. H**.
MONTESOL. Vara de Rey, 2. HR**.
NÁUTICO EBESO. Ramón Muntaner, 44. H**.
BENJAMÍN. Talamanca, s/n. H*.
FIGUERETAS. Playa Figueretas, s/n. H*.
ISLA. Ses Figueres. H*.
MARE NOSTRUM. Playa d'en Bossa, s/n. H*.
MARIGNA. Al Sabini, s/n. H*.
MARÍTIMO. Ramón Muntaner, s/n. HR*.
NORAY. Eugenio Molina, 14. H*.
PALAU. Galicia, 12. H*.
SES FIGUERES. Barriada de Ses Figueres, s/n. H*.
DON PEPE. Avda. Bartolomé V. Ramón, 24. HA**.
LAS PALMERAS. Calle Catorce, s/n. HA**.
EL CORSARIO. Poniente, 5. H**.
ES VIVE. Barriada Es Vive. H**.
INTERNACIONAL. Ctra. Ibiza-San Juan, km. 2. H**.
PARQUE. Cayetano Soler. HR**.
PITYUSA. Galicia, 29. HR**.
ROCAMAR. Talamanca, s/n. H**.
TALAMANCA. Playa Talamanca. H**.
URSA. Galicia, s/n. HR**.
AVENIDA. Avda. Bartolomé V. Ramón, 26. HR*.
COMERCIO. Olozaga, 11. P*.
DALT MAR. Los Molinos. HR*.
EBUSITANIA. Obispo Huix, s/n. HR*.
ESPAÑA. Avda. Bartolomé V. Ramón, 1. H*.
FORMENTERA. Pl. José Pidal, 5. HR*.
JUANITO. Juan de Austria, 17. HR*.
MAR BLAU. Los Molinos. H*.
MONERRIS. Barrio Escandell. H*.
LAS NIEVES. Juan de Austria, 19. HR*.
OLIVER. Ignacio Riquer, 12. H*.
OSUNA. Obispo Huix, 12. HR*.
RIPOL. Vicente Cuervo, 12. HR*.
SOL Y BRISA. Avda. Bartolomé V. Ramón, 15. HR*.

Cala Llonga (Santa Eulalia del Río)

PLAYA DORADA. H**.
TONI. H*.

Cala Nova

CALA NOVA. H**.

Es Caná (Santa Eulalia del Río)

ÁNFORA PLAYA. Playa Es Cana. H**.
ATLANTIC. Playa Es Caná. H**.
ERESO. Playa Es Caná. H*.
PINOMAR. Es Caná, 99. H*.
LAS ARENAS. Playa Es Caná. H**.
FLAMINGO. H**.
MAR Y HUERTA. Playa Es Caná. H**.
PERLA. Playa Es Caná. H**.
PLAYA SOL. Playa. HR**.
LOS PINOS. Es Caná, s/n. H*.
PUNTA ARABI. CV**.

Figueretas

COPACABANA. Ramón Muntaner. H**.
DON QUIJOTE. Alava, s/n. H**.
VICTORIA. Playa Ses Figueres. H**.

Los Molinos

MUNTANER. Ramón Muntaner, 55. HR*.

Portinatx (San Juan)

EL GRECO. H**.
PRESIDENTE-PLAYA. Playa de Portinatx. H**.
CAS MALLORQUI. Playa Portinatx, 28. H**.
OASIS. Playa Portinatx. H**.
LA CIGÜEÑA. H*.
PORTINATX. Carretera, 28. H*.
SE VINYE. HR*.

San Agustín (San José)

BERGANTÍN. Playa S'Estanyol. H***.
ELS PINS. Cala de Bou. H***.
RIVERA. Can Lluch. H**.
TAGOMAGO. Playa S'Estanyol. H**.
ELSA. Ses Fontanelles, s/n. HR**.

San Antonio Abad

PALMYRA. Doctor Fleming, s/n. H****.
ABRAT. El Cals del Moro. H***.
ACOR. Cala Gració. H***.
ARENAL. Doctor Fleming. H***.
BAHÍA. Bellavista. H***.
BELLAMAR. Playa Es Puet. H***.
CALA GRACIÓ. Playa de Cala Gració, s/n. H***.
COLINA. Balanzat, 13. H***.
COLUMBUS. Punta Xinxo. H***.
HAWAI. Punta Des Moli. H***.
HELIOS. Playa S'Estanyol. H***.
MARCO POLO. Ctra. Ibiza-San Antonio. H***.
NEPTUNO. Bellavista Punta de Molino, 2. H***.
PINET PLAYA. Bahía de San Antonio. H***.
SAN DIEGO. Bahía de San Antonio. H***.
TROPICAL. Cervantes, s/n. H***.
BRISA. Valencia, s/n. H**.

ES PLA. Ctra. Ibiza-San Antonio, 12. H**.
FLORIDA. Ramón y Cajal, 2. H**.
GRAN SOL. Es Calo Des Moro. H**.
MONTBLANCH. Mar, 1. H**.
PACIFIC. Ctra. Ibiza-San Antonio, km 15. H**.
PISCIS. Miramar, s/n. H**.
S'ANFORA. Ctra. San José. H**.
SES SEVINES. Playa San Antonio. H**.
CATALINA. Balanzat, 54. H*.
COVES BLANQUES. San Antonio, s/n. H*.
DON JUAN. Santa Inés, 7. HR*.
EXCELSIOR. Vara de Rey, 17. H*.
GALERA. San Vicente, s/n. HR*.
GALFI. Avda. Doctor Fleming, s/n. H*.
LLEVANT. Ramón y Cajal, 9. HR*.
MARCH. Ctra. San Antonio-Ibiza, km 14. H*.
MARFIL. Ramón y Cajal, s/n. H*.
MITJORN. Camino del Faro, 10. HR*.
OROSOL. Ramón y Cajal, s/n. H*.
PORTMANY. Belanzat, 12. HR*.
SALADA. Soledad, s/n. HR*.
VEDRA. Del Mar, 7. H*.
OSIRIS. Playa San Antonio. H***.
RECO DES SOL. Bosch Den Frit. H***.
SES ALAMERAS. Ctra. de Ibiza, 15. H***.
APOLO. Mañanet, s/n. H**.
ATALAYA. San Bartolomé, s/n. H**.
CERVANTES. Mahón, s/n. H**.
ESMERALDA. Progreso, 3. H**.
FLEMING. Avda. Doctor Fleming, 67. H**.
GRAN PARAÍSO. Cas Vergé. H**.
MALLORCA. Mallorca, 9. H**.
NORTE. Santa Rosalía, s/n. H**.
PUCHET. Avda. Doctor Fleming, 6. H**.
ROCA. San Mateo, 11. H**.
ROSALÍA. Santa Rosalía, 11. H**.
SAN ANTONIO. Mira Mar, 7. HR**.
SÁNCHEZ. Can Obrador. H**.
TARBA. Ramón y Cajal, 10. H**.
TORRES. Soledad, 34. H**.
VALENCIA. Valencia, s/n. HR**.
ADELINO. Alicante, s/n. H*.
ALICANTE. Alicante, s/n. H*.
CISNE. Vara de Rey, 13. HR*.
ESTRELLA DEL MAR. Vedra, s/n. H*.
FERRER. Obispo Torres, 5. H*.
FLORENCIO. Soledad, 42. H*.
FLORES. Rusell, 26. HR*.
HORIZONTE. Progreso, s/n. HR*.
LAUREL. Marino Riquer, s/n. HR*.
MANOLITA. Progreso, s/n. HR*.
MARI. Progreso, 36. H*.
MARICEL. Playa San Antonio. Avda. Doctor Fleming. H*.
MARILINA. Camino del Faro, s/n. HR*.
MONTE MAR. San Antonio, 46. H*.
MOTO LUIS. Ctra. Ibiza-San Antonio, 15. HR*.
NICOLAU. Santa Rosalía, s/n. HR*.
RITA. Mallorca, 5. HR*.
ROIG. Progreso, 38. HR*.
SALA. Soledad, 18. HR*.
SIRENA. Vedra, s/n. HR*.

11

LA TORRE. Cap. Negret. H*.
VALL PUIG. Progreso, s/n. HR*.
VISTA ALEGRE. Ramón y Cajal, s/n. HR*.

San Francisco (San José)

CODOLA. Playa de Codola. H*.

San José

CAP NONO. Les Forilanelles. H***.
DON TONI. Playa d'en Bossa. H***.
MILORD. Punta Xinxo. H***.
PLAYA D'EN BOSSA. Playa d'en Bossa. H***.
SAN REMO. Playa S'Estanyol. H***.
S'ESTANYOL. Playa S'Estanyol. H***.
TAMPICO. Bahía de San Antonio. H***.
IBIZA PUEBLO. Port Des Torrent. H*.
CA'N BOSSA. Playa d'en Bossa. H**.
MAR Y SAL. La Canal. H*.
SA PALMERA. La Canal. H*.

San Juan Bautista

HACIENDA NA XAMENA. Urbanización Na Xamena. H****.
IMPERIO PLAYA. Cala San Vicente. H***.
CALA SAN VICENTE. Playa Cala San Vicente. H**.
CIGUEÑA PLAYA. Cala Portinatx. H*.

San Miguel (San Juan Bautista)

CARTAGO. Playa Port Des Turrent. H***.
GALEÓN. Puerto de San Miguel. H***.

Santa Eulalia del Río

FENICIA. Ca'n Fita. H****.
AUGUSTA. Urbanización Sargamasa. H***.
CALA LLONGA. Playa Cala Llonga. H***.
DON CARLOS. Urbanización Siesta. H***.
MIAMI. Playa Es Caná. H***.
PANORAMA. Es Caná. H***.
S'ARGAMASA. Urbanización S'Argamasa. H***.
SES ESTAQUES. Ses Estaques. H***.
SIESTA. Urbanización Siesta. H***.
TRES TORRES. Ses Estaques. H***.
CARIBE. Playa Es Caná. H**.
CORAL PLAYA. Playa Es Caná. H**.
ES CANÁ PLAYA. Playa de Es Caná. H**.
RIOMAR. Playa Pins, s/n. H**.
ARABI. Ctra. de San Carlos, s/n. HR*.
LA CALA. San Jaime, s/n. H*.
MEDITERRÁNEO. Calle H o Camino de Misas, s/n. H*.
EL PINAR. Playa Cala Llonga, s/n. HR*.
SES ROQUES. Del Mar, s/n. H*.
BUENAVISTA. San Jaime, s/n. H**.
CAS CATALA. Camino de la Iglesia, s/n. HR*.
ES PUJOLET. San Jaime, s/n. H*.
GIROS. San Jaime, s/n. HR*.
MARCH. San Lorenzo, s/n. H**.
MARSOL. Playa Dels Pins, s/n. HR**.

REY. San José, s/n. H**.
YEBISAU. Paseo del Generalísimo, s/n. H**.
CASA PEPE. Es Caná, s/n. H*.
CENTRAL. San Vicente, s/n. H*.
LOS HERMANOS. San Vicente, s/n. HR*.
LA PILARICA. Avda. General Franco. HR*.
SA ROTA. San Vicente, s/n. HR*.
SANTA EULALIA. San Jaime, s/n. HR*.

Talamanca

EL CORSO. Isla Plana, s/n. H***.
PLAYA REAL. H**.

Formentera

FORMENTERA PLAYA. H***.
CALA SAHONA. Cala Sahona, s/n. H**.
CASBAH MITJORN. H**.
ENTREPINOS. Es Calo-Nuestra Señora del Pilar. H**.
CA-MARI. Playa Mitjorn, s/n. P*.
ITALIA. HR*.
SANTI. Playa Mitjorn. H*.
TAHITÍ. Playa Es Pujols, s/n. H*.

Sabina (La)

BELLAVISTA. Puerto de La Sabina. H*.
LAGO DORADO. Puerto La Sabina. H*.

San Fernando

ROCABELLA. Playa Es Pujols, s/n. H*.
CALMA. Playa Es Pujols, s/n. H**.
ROCAPLANA. Playa Es Pujols, s/n. H**.
VORAMAR. Playa Es Pujols. H**.
ALEMANIA. Playa Es Pujols. HR*.
CAPRI. Playa Es Pujols, s/n. H*.
LEVANTE. Playa Es Pujols, s/n. HR*.
MAYANS. Can Manuel Tauet Camp Des Batle. HR*.
PEPE. H*.
LOS ROSALES. Playa Es Pujols, s/n. H*.
ROSAMAR. Playa Es Pujols, s/n. H*.
SA ROQUETA. Playa Es Pujols, s/n. H*.

San Francisco Javier

SOL Y MAR. Playa Mitjorn, s/n. HR*.

2.2. **APARTAMENTOS TURÍSTICOS**
APPARTEMENTS TOURISTIQUES
TOURIST APARTMENTS
APARTEMENTHAUSER

Ibiza

CAN BOSSA. Playa D'en Bossa. 1.ª C.
CARIBE. Playa Figueretas. 3.ª C.
CASA EUROPA. Talamanca. 3.ª C.
DALTMAR. Formentera, 3. 2.ª C.
DELFÍN VERDE (EL). Garijo, 3. 3.ª C.

EXTREMADURA. Playa de Ses Figueres. 3.ª C.
FREUS. Ramón Muntaner, 25. 2.ª C.
GRAN SOL. Formentera, 7. 3.ª C.
HERAS (LAS). Navarra, s/n. 2.ª C.
MARIÁNGELES. Galicia, 8. 2.ª C.
MILFLORES. Playa D'en Bossa. 3.ª C.
MIL VISTES. Los Molinos, s/n. 3.ª C.
PUNTA DE DALT (LA). Playa D'en Bossa. 3.ª C.
ROSELLO. Los Molinos. 3.ª C.
SA TANCA. Los Molinos. 1.ª C.
VILAS. Es Vivé. 1.ª C.
VILLA MITJORN. Calle Treinta y siete, s/n.
   3.ª C.

Figueretas

LEDESMA. Es Vivé (Figueretas). 2.ª C.
LENOIR. Galicia, s/n. 3.ª C.
PITUSA. Galicia, s/n. 3.ª C.

San Antonio Abad

ALBARES (LOS). Vara de Rey. 1.ª C.
BAHÍA BLAVA. Balanzat, 24. 3.ª C.
CASA BLANCA. Balanzat, s/n. 3.ª C.
CHABUSA. Playa S'Estanyol. 3.ª C.
INMOBILIARIA NEPTUNO, S. A. Cala de Bou.-
   S'Estanyol. 1.ª C.
MATUR. Balanset, 34. 2.ª C.
MEDITERRÁNEO. Santa Inés, 1. 1.ª C.
PLAYA GRASIO. 3.ª C.
PUNTAS VARIADAS. Punta Ses Variades. 3.ª C.
SES FUNTANELLAS. Ctra. Port del Turrent.
   3.ª C.
S'ILLA BLANCA. Avda. Doctor Fleming, s/n.
   3.ª C.
TORRE (LA). Cap. Negret. 3.ª C.

San Carlos (Santa Eulalia)

ARENAL D'OR. Es Figueral. 3.ª C.
BUNGALOWS PARK. Es Figueral. 2.ª C.
ES CANÁ. Playa Es Caná. 3.ª C.

Santa Eulalia

CAN USINA. Playa Es Caná. 3.ª C.
CIUDAD DE VACACIONES PUNTA ARABÍ.
   Punta Arabí. 2.ª C.
PINOSOL. Barrio Can Museña. 3.ª C.
SAMSO. Sa Caleta. 3.ª C.
SIESTA. Urbanización Siesta. 1.ª C.

San José

ANÍBAL. Playa Es Codolar. 1.ª C.
MEGO. Cala Bou. 2.ª C.
NORIA (LA). Playa D'en Bossa. 2.ª C.

Formentera

GAVIOTA (LA). Playa Es Calo. 3.ª C.
MERIDIUM. Playa Mitjorn. 3.ª C.
REDOS. Playa Mitjorn. 3.ª C.

2.3. CAMPINGS

San Antonio Abad

SAN ANTONIO. Ctra. Ibiza, km 14. 2.ª C.
CALA BASSA. Final ctra. de Ibiza-Cala Bassa.
   3.ª C.
FLORIDA. Punta Arabí, Santa Eulalia.

3. GASTRONOMÍA
GASTRONOMIE
GASTRONOMY
GASTRONOMIE

3.1. RESTAURANTES
RESTAURANTS
RESTAURANTS
RESTAURANTS

Ibiza

AEROPUERTO. Aeropuerto Nacional de Ibiza.
CELLER BALEAR. Ignacio Wallis, 18.
ES GRILL. Tagomago, s/n.
ALFREDO. Vara de Rey, 16.
BALEARES. Ramón Muntaner, 12.
EL BARCO BORRACHO. Playa de Bossa, s/n.
CARTAGO. Vía Púnica, 8.
DELFÍN VERDE. Garijo, 2.
FILIPPO. Plaza Garijo, 5.
FORMENTERA. Eugenio Molina, 4.
SOCIEDAD DEPORTIVA IBIZA. Juan de Aus-
   tria, 10.

La Calobra

TORRENTE DE PAREIS. La Calobra.

San Antonio Abad

R. CAPRI. Avda. Doctor Fleming, s/n.
CELLER EL REFUGIO. Bartolomé Vicente Ra-
   món, 5.
CONTINENTAL. Balanzat, 24.
BIBLOS CLUB. Santa Inés, 1.
CELLER ES CUBELL. Ramón y Cajal, s/n.
CORTIJO TRISTÁN. San Antonio, 11.
ES VEDRA. Miramar, s/n.
PARÍS. Progreso, 28.
RAMÓN. San Vicente, 55.
S'OLIVER. San Mateo, 9.

San Carlos

LAS DALIAS. Ctra. Santa Eulalia, s/n.

San Jorge

CAN TIXEDO. Ctra. La Canal, s/n.
CAN JURAT. Can Jurat.

San José

CALA VADELLA. Cala Vadella.
SES FUNTANELLAS. Ctra. Port del Turrent, s/n.
CAN MAÑANET. Can Mañanet.
SA COVA SANTA. Ctra. San José-Ibiza, km 2.

San Juan Bautista

PINOS PLAYA. Playa Portinatx.

San Miguel

SES OLIVERAS. Puerto San Miguel.

Santa Eulalia del Río

DEL MAR. Cala Llonga.
MIRANDA. Playa Es Caná.
SA CALETA. San Jaime, s/n.
SA PUNTA. Santa Eulalia del Río, s/n.
CALA LLONGA. Playa de Cala Llonga, s/n.
CELLER CAN PERA. San Jaime, s/n.
ES CANAR. Playa de Es Canar.
LOS ESPÁRRAGOS SILVESTRES. Playa Cala
    Llonga.
ES PRENSO. Ramón Muntaner, 43.
PURCHETS. Playa Cala Llonga.

Formentera

CAN RAFAI. Can Rafai.
DES PEIX. Calles P y H. La Sabina.
ES ARENALS. Playa Mitjorn.
LA PÉRGOLA. Playa Es Pujols.
CHEZ-GERDI. Es Pujols.
PEYKA. San Fernando.
PLAYA. Playa Es Pujols.
LOS ROSALES. Playa Es Pujols.
SAN FERNANDO. San Fernando, s/n.
SE CALA. Nuestra Señora del Pilar, s/n.

3.2. ESPECIALIDADES GASTRONÓMICAS
    SPÉCIALITÉS GASTRONOMIQUES
    GASTRONOMIC SPECIALITIES
    SPEZIALITÄTEN GASTRONOMISCHE

Bebidas: Existen unos licores típicos hechos
    con hierbas, entre los que destacan la frí-
    gola, romany y «Hierbas».
Burrida de ratjada. Raya con salsa de almen-
    dras.
Tortuga. Guiso de tortuga con legumbres.
Dentón o mero al horno. Asado con salsa de
    perejil, cebolla y tomate.
Sofrit pages. Fritura de cordero, cerdo y pollo
    con hortalizas.
Pabrassus a la brasa. Setas parrilla con picada
    de perejil, ajo y pan rallado.
Repostería y dulces. «Oreietes», «Macarrones
    de San Juan», «Grarxonera», «Flaó», «Bes-
    cuit», «Salsa de Nadal».

Boissons: il y a des liqueurs typiques faites
    avec des herbes parmi lesquelles nous pou-
    vons signaler la «frigola», «romany» et «her-
    bes».

Bourride de ratjada. Raie avec sauce aux
    amendes.
Tortue. Tortue assaisonnée avec légumes.
Denton ou merou au four. Grillé avec sauce au
    persil, oignon et tomate.
Sofrit pages. Friture de poulet, agneau et porc
    avec primeurs.
Pabrassus a la braise. Champignons au grill
    avec un peu de persil, d'ail et de pain râpé.
Dessert et confiserie. «Oreietes», «Macarrons
    de Saint Jean», «Grarxonera», «Flaó»,
    «Bes-Cuit», «Sauce de Nadal».

Drinks: There exist typical liqueurs made with
    herbs, among which «frígola», «romany» and
    «hierbas» are prominent.
Burrida de ratjada. Skate-fish with almond
    sauce.
Turtle: Turtle and vegetable stew.
Baked porgy or black grouper: Baked with
    parsley, onion and tomato sauce.
Sofrit pages: Lamb, pig and chiken fry with ve-
    getables.
Pabrassus a la brasa: Broiled mushrooms with
    chopped parsley, garlic and grated bread.
Pastries and sweets: «Oreietes», «Saint John
    Macaroni», «Grarxonera», «Flaó», «Bescuit»,
    «Salsa de Nadal» (Christmas Sauce).

Getränke: Es gibt verschiedene Liköre, die aus
    Kräutern hergestellt werden, und typisch für
    Ibiza sind: «Frigola», «Romany» und «Hier-
    bas» (Kräuter).
Burrida de ratjada: Rochen mit Mandelsosse.
Tortuga: Gerich aus Schildkröte und Gemüse.
Denton o mero al horno. Gebratene Fisch mit
    einer Sosse aus Petersilie, Zwiebeir und To-
    maten.
Sofrit pages. Gericht aus Hammel, Schweir und
    Huhn mit Gemüse.
Pabrassus a la brasa. Ein Gericht aus einer be-
    summten gebratenen Pilzsorte mit Petersilie,
    Knoblauch und geriebenem Brot.
Sussigkeiten. «Oreietes», «Macarrones de San
    Juan», «Grarxonera», «Flaó», «Bes-cuit»,
    «Salsa de Nadal».

4. AGENDA PRÁCTICA
    AGENDA PRATIQUE
    PRACTICAL AGENDA
    PRAKTISCHES NACHSCHLA-
    GEWERK

4.1. CONSULADOS
    CONSULATS
    CONSULATES
    KONSULATE

Ibiza

VICECONSULADO BRITÁNICO. B. Roselló, 24,
    9.º.

VICECONSULADO DE FRANCIA. Avenida España, 1.
VICECONSULADO DE HOLANDA. Vía Púnica, 2-B.
VICECONSULADO DE ITALIA. B. V. Ramón, 32, 1.º.
VICECONSULADO DE SUECIA. Castelar, 12.

San Antonio

VICECONSULADO DE ALEMANIA. Apartamentos El Patio. Calle Miramar.

4.2. DIRECCIONES Y SERVICIOS ÚTILES
ADRESSES ET SERVICES UTILES
USEFUL ADDRESSES AND SERVICES
NOTZLICHE ADRESSEN UND DIENSTE

**Correos. Postes.
Post Offices. Postamter**

Madrid, s/n. Ibiza.

**Telégrafos. Télégraphes
Telegraph Offices. Telegraphenämter**

Madrid, s/n. Ibiza.

**Teléfonos. Téléphones.
Telephone Exchanges. Telephonamt**

Aragón, s/n. Ibiza.

**Teléfonos de urgencia
Téléphones d'urgence
Emergency telephone numbers
Notrute**

SERVICIO MÉDICO DE URGENCIA. Telf. 30 31 31. Ibiza.
CASA DE SOCORRO. Telf. 30 11 83. Ibiza.
SEGURIDAD SOCIAL. Telf. 30 02 00. Ibiza.
BOMBEROS. Telf. 30 11 71. Ibiza.
GUARDIA CIVIL. Telf. 30 11 95. Ibiza.
POLICÍA NACIONAL. Telf. 30 11 31. Ibiza.

**Comunicaciones
Communications
Communications
Verkehrsverbindungen**

Aubobuses. Autobus. Buses. Buslinien

Parada de autobús: Avda. Isidoro Macabich, Ibiza.
Existen las siguientes líneas de autobuses: Ibiza-San Antonio, a Santa Eulalia, a San Juan, a San José, a San Carlos, a San Miguel, a San Rafael, a Santa Inés y a San Mateo.

Durante el verano existen líneas a las principales playas de la isla.

**Talleres de reparación de automóviles. (Agencias Oficiales.)
Ateliers de reparation d'automobiles. (Agences Officielles.)
Car repair garages. (Oficial Agencies.)
Autoreparaturwerkstatten. (Offizielle Agenturen.)**

GARAGE ADROVER. Avda. España, 22. Especialidad Ford.
RENAULT. Servicio Oficial. Ctra. San José, km 2.
CITROËN. Servicio Oficial B. V. Ramón, 20.
SEAT. Servicio Oficial. Madrid, s/n.
GARAGE VIDAL. Abad y La Sierra, 39. Servicio Oficial: DKW, Mercedes, Morris, Austin, Volkswagen.
TALLER ORDINAS. Ctra. San Juan, km 1,2. Servicio Oficial de Simca.

**Información sobre el estado de las carreteras
Renseignement sur l'état des routes
Information on road conditions
Auskunft über den Zustand der Landstrassen**

TELERRUTA M. O. P. (cinta grabada). Telfs. (91) 254 28 00 y (91) 254 50 05. Estado de carreteras y puertos por temporales de nieves y lluvias, y posibles desvíos por obras. Servicio permanente.
Información general del pavimento, distancias y caminos más convenientes para un determinado itinerario, llamar al teléfono (91) 253 16 00, solicitando el Servicio «no grabado» de Telerruta. Horario, invierno, de 8,30 a 22 horas; verano, de 8,30 a 20,30 horas.

**Líneas aéreas-Lignes aeriennes
Air lines-Luftfahrtgesellschaften**

Con Alicante. En verano, tres vuelos semanales.
Con Barcelona. De dos a tres vuelos diarios.
Con Palma de Mallorca. De dos a tres vuelos diarios.
Con Valencia. De uno a dos vuelos diarios.
Con Madrid. De uno a dos vuelos a la semana.
Con Londres. Cuatro vuelos a la semana.
Con Frankfurt. Cuatro vuelos semanales, vía Barcelona.
Con París. En verano, un vuelo diario.
Con Bruselas. En verano, un vuelo diario.
IBERIA. Vara de Rey, 15. Aeropuerto.
AVIACO. Avda. Bartolomé V. Ramón, 1.

BUA (BRITISH UNITED AIRWAYS). Galerías Serra. Paseo Vara de Rey.

Lineas maritimas
Lignes maritimas
Maritimes lines
Schiffahrtsgesellschaften

Con Barcelona. De uno a siete barcos semanales.
Con Palma de Mallorca. De tres a seis barcos semanales.
Con Valencia. De dos a tres barcos semanales.
Con Alicante. De dos a tres barcos semanales.
Con Formentera. Varios servicios al día.
Con Málaga. Un barco semanal (de marzo a octubre).
Con Génova. Un barco semanal (de marzo a octubre).
TRASMEDITERRÁNEA. Bartolomé Vicente Ramón, 2. Consignataria de la compañía francesa Paquet.
HIJOS DE ABEL MATUTES TORRES. Agentes generales de D. F. D. S. Seaways, Vara de Rey, 1.
NAVIERA FORMENTERA. Bartolomé Vicente Ramón, 8.
NAVIERA MALLORQUINA. Edificio Bahía.
COMPAGNIE MIXTE DE NAVIGATION. Eugenio Molina, 12.

Formentera

El acceso a Formentera se realiza a través de Ibiza, que mantiene un nutrido servicio aéreo y marítimo con diversas capitales de la península y con Palma de Mallorca.
Entre Ibiza y Formentera funciona una línea marítima que efectúa de uno a tres viajes diarios. Este servicio se combina con otro de autobuses que pone en contacto La Sabina, San Francisco y La Mola.

L'accès à Formentera se fait par Ibiza qui dispose d'un service aérien et maritime dense avec les différentes villes de la Péninsule et Palma de Mallorca.
Entre Ibiza et Formentera, il y a une ligne maritime qui effectue un à trois voyages par jour. Ce service se combine avec celui des autobuses qui relie La Sabina, San Francisco et La Mola.

Acces to Formentera is by way of Ibiza, which has a very good sea and air service with various capitals in the Peninsula and with Palma de Mallorca.
Between Ibiza and Formentera there is a sea line making from one to three trips a day. This service combines with buses getting into contact with La Sabina, San Francisco and La Mola.

Man hat Zugang nach Formentera über Ibiza, die zahlreiche Luftund Seeverbindungen mit verschiedenen Städten der Halbinsel und mit Palma de Mallorca aufweist.
Zwischen Ibiza und Formentera besteht eine Schiffsverbindung. die täglich 1-3 Über fahrten durchführt. Dieser Dienst wird mit einem autobusverkehr verbunden, der La Sabina, San Francisco und La Mola berührt.

5. FIESTAS Y ESPECTÁCULOS
FÊTES ET SPECTACLES
FESTIVITIES AND SPECTACLES
FESTE UND SCHAUSPIELE

5.1. CLUBS Y SOCIEDADES DEPORTIVAS
CLUBS ET SOCIÉTÉS SPORTIVES
CLUBS AND SPORTS SOCIETES
CLUBS UND SPORTCLUBS

EBUSUS. Paseo de Vara de Rey, 20. Ibiza.
CASINO DE IBIZA. Andenes del Puerto. Ibiza.
CLUB NÁUTICO. Astilleros. Ibiza.
SOCIEDAD DE CAZADORES. José Antonio, 5. Ibiza.
SOCIEDAD COLOMBÓFILA. Conde de Roselló, 3. Ibiza.
SOCIEDAD TANIT. Avda. España. Ibiza.
CENTRO INICIATIVAS Y TURISMO. Vía Romana, 8.
TENIS CLUB. Avda. España, s/n.

Piscinas-Piscines
Swimming Pools
Schwimmbader

Carretera de San Juan, s/n. Ibiza.

5.2. CAZA
CHASSE
HUNTING
JAGD

De octubre a febrero, conejos, perdices, tórtolas, codornices y otras aves silvestres. La veda para aves acuáticas empieza el 1 de mayo. Hay una Sociedad de Cazadores y otra Colombófila.

5.3. ESPECTÁCULOS-SPECTACLES
SHOWS-SCHAUSPIELE

Salas de fiestas-Cabarets
Nigh clubs-Tanziokale

MAR BLAU. Los Molinos. Ibiza.
PACHA. P.º Marítimo. Talamanca. Ibiza.

SACROMONTE. Playa d'En Bossa. Ibiza.
ISLA BLANCA. Avda. del Dr. Fleming, s/n. San Antonio.
NITO'S CLUB. Santa Inés, s/n. San Antonio.
SA TANCA. Ctra. San Antonio-Ibiza. San Antonio.
SAN FRANCISCO. Soledad, 42. San Antonio.
ES XARC. Desembocadura río. Santa Eulalia.
LA CANCELA. Es Caná. Santa Eulalia.
COVA SANTA. Ctra. Ibiza-San José, San José.
MAGOO. Es Pujols. Formentera.
GLORY'S. Can Bufi. Ctra. Ibiza-San Antonio. Ibiza.
L'ANFORA. San Carlos, 5. Ibiza.
NEW LOLA'S. Alfonso XIII, s/n. Ibiza.
PORTAL NOU. Portal Nou. Ibiza.
TIKI. Navarra, 11. Ibiza.
XALOC. Navarra, 28. Ibiza.
AMNESIA. Ctra. Ibiza-San Antonio, km 5.
CHARC-MOOL. C. de Mar. San Antonio.
CLUB SAN RAFAEL. Ctra. Ibiza-San Antonio, km 6.
DINOS CLUB. San Antonio.
ES PARADIS TERRENAL. Travesía Miramar, 5. San Antonio.
ÉXTASIS. Miramar, s/n. San Antonio.
KONTIKI. San Antonio.
PLAY BOY CLUB. Avda. del Dr. Fleming. San Antonio.
PLAY BOY 2. San Antonio, esquina Santa Inés. San Antonio.
ZOOM ZOOM. B. V. Ramón. San Antonio.
BOUCALA. Ctra. Port des Tourrent. San José.
LAS RANAS. Cala Vadella. San José.
AL SABINI. Santa Eulalia.
CAN MALA-COSTA. Santa Eulalia.
CORTIJO. Es Caná. Santa Eulalia.
JOVIS. Cala Llonga. Santa Eulalia.
REVOLUTION. Es Caná. Santa Eulalia.
SES PARRES. San Jaime. Santa Eulalia.
SNOOPY. Es Caná. Santa Eulalia.
LAS DALIAS. San Carlos.
TISUHÉ CLUB. Portinatx. San Juan.
BARBACOA SAN ANTONIO.
BARBACOA IBIZA. Santa Gertrudis.
BARBACOA COVA SANTA. San José.

Plazas de toros
Arènes-Bullrings
Stierkampfarenas

En verano se celebran varias corridas en la plaza de toros de Ibiza, cuyo aforo es de 4 000 plazas. Los lunes, fiesta campera o corrida de toros, durante los meses de abril a octubre.

Durant l'été ont lieu plusieurs corridas aux arènes d'Ibiza qui a 4 000 places. Entre avril et octobre, les lundis il y a fête en pleinair ou des corridas pour amateurs.

In the summer, several bullfights are held in the bullring in Ibiza, seating 4 000 people. On Mondays, heifer-fighting festivals or bullfights, from April through October.

Im Sommer, inde verschiedene Stierkämpfe in der Arena von Ibiza stätt, die 4 000 Plätze aufvreist. Während der Monate April bis Oktober findet montags eine «Fiesta campera» under ein Stierkampf stätt.

6. TURISMO

6.1. EXCURSIONES A LOS ALREDEDORES DE IBIZA
EXCURSIONS AUX ENVIRONS D'IBIZA
EXCURSIONS ROUND AND ABOUT IBIZA
AUSFLUGE IN DIE UMGEBUNG IBIZA

DE IBIZA A SAN ANTONIO
D'IBIZA A SAN ANTONIO
IBIZA TO SAN ANTONIO
VON IBIZA NACH SAN ANTONIO

Recorriendo la villa, la hermosa bahía y Cala Gració, continuando hacia San José para visitar las exhibiciones folklóricas y la «Cueva Santa»; regresando a Ibiza directamente o desviándose antes hacia Las Salinas, en La Canal.

Parcourir la ville, la très belle baie et Cala Gració, aller vers San José pour visiter les expositioris folkloriques et la «Grotte Sainte»; revenir directement à Ibiza ou faire un détour auparavant vers Las Salinas et La Canal.

Traveling through the villa, the beautiful bay and Cala Gració, continuing to San José to visit the folklore exhibitions and the «Cueva Santa» (Holy Cave), returning to Ibiza directly or going previously toward Las Salinas in La Canal.

Wir fahren durch die Stadt, vorbei an der schönen Bucht und Cala Gració, fahren weiter nach San José, um die folkloristischen Darbietungen und die «Cueva Santa» zu besuchen. Wir kehren entweder direkt nach Ibiza zurück oder machen einen Abstecher vorher nach Las Salinas in La Canal.

DE IBIZA A CALA LLONGA
D'IBIZA A CALA LLONGA
IBIZA TO CALA LLONGA
VON IBIZA NACH CALA LLONGA

Continuando hacia Santa Eulalia del Río, visitando la villa y su interesante iglesia fortaleza del «Puig de Missa» y siguiendo luego hasta la deliciosa playa de Es Canar.

En passant par Santa Eulalia del Río, il faut visiter la ville et son intéressante église forteresse du «Puig de Missa» et suivre ensuite pour arriver à la charmante plage de Es Canar.

Continuing toward Santa Eulalia del Río, visiting the village and its interesting church-fortress of «Puig de Missa» following later up to the beautiful Es Canar beach.

Wir fahren nach Santa Eulalia del Río, besichtigen die Stadt und die interessante befestigte Kirche des «Puig de Missa» und fahren später weiter zu dem wunderbaren Strand Es Canar.

DE IBIZA A SAN JUAN Y A LAS HERMOSAS CALAS «XARRACA» Y «PORTINATX»
D'IBIZA A SAN JUAN ET AUX BELLES CALAS «XARRACA» ET «PORTINATX»
IBIZA TO SAN JUAN AND THE BEAUTIFUL «XARRACA» AND «PORTINATX» COVES
VON IBIZA NACH SAN JUAN UND DEN HÜBSCHEN BUCHTEN «XARRACA» UND «PORTINATX»

Deteniéndose a la ida o al regreso en el poblado de Balafi.

S'arrêter à l'allée et au retour dans le village de Balafi.

Stopping, going or coming back, in Balafi village.

Auf der Hin und Rückfahrt marchen wir einen Halt im Dorf Balafi.

En los meses de verano se pueden efectuar excursiones en lancha. Desde Ibiza, a Talamanca. Desde San Antonio a Cala Bassa, Port d'Es Torrent y a Es Vedrá. Desde Santa Eulalia a la playa de Es Canar y Cala Llonga.

En été, on peut faire des excursions en barque. D'Ibiza à Talamanca. De San Antonio à Cala Bassa. Port d'Es Torrent et à Es Vedrá. De Santa Eulalia à la plage de Es Canar et Cala Llonga.

In the summer months motor-boat tours can be made. From Ibiza, to Talamanca. From San Antonio, to Cala Bassa, Port d'Es Torrent and to Es Vedrá. From Santa Eulalia, to Es Canar beach and Cala Llonga.

In den Sommermonaten kann man Ausflüge im Motorboot unternehmen. Von Ibiza nach Talamanca. Von San Antonio nach Cala Bassa, Port dës Torrent und nach Es Vedrá. Von Santa Eulalia aus zu dem Strand Es Canar und Cala Llonga.

Formentera

La visita a Formentera reviste gran interés. La travesía en lancha a través del paso de Los Freos es de unos 45 minutos. En Formentera merece especial atención la visita a La Mola, Cala Sahona y la playa de Es Pujols.

La visite de Formentera revêt un grand intérêt. La traversée en barque par le passage des Los Freos dure environ 45 mn. Il faut voir tout particulièrement La Mola, Cala Sahona et la plage d'Es Pujols.

The visit to Formentera is very interesting. The trip by motor-boat through the Los Freos pass is about 45 minutes. In Formentera, special attention is deserved by a visit to La Mola, Cala Sahona and Es Pujols beach.

Es ist sehr interessant Formentera zu besuchen. Die überfahrt in einem Motorboot durch die Meerenge Los Freos dauert 45 Minuten. Auf Formentera sollte man vorallem La Mola, Cala Sahona und den Strand Es Pujols besuchen.

6.2. POBLACIONES IMPORTANTES
VILLAGES IMPORTANTS
IMPORTANT TOWNS
BEDEUTENDE ORTE

San Antonio Abad

Se halla al oeste de Ibiza, a 16 km de la capital y frente a la isla Conejera. Tiene la villa unos 1 500 habitantes. Su hermosa bahía, que los romanos llamaron «Portus Magnus», es uno de los lugares predilectos del turismo. En las cercanías de la villa se encuentra la catacumba o capilla subterránea de Santa Inés, declarada Monumento Nacional, y la cueva «Ses Fontanelles», donde pueden admirarse unas interesantes pinturas rupestres.

Ce village est situé à l'ouest d'Ibiza, à 16 km de la capitale et face à l'île Conejera. Il compte autour de 1 500 habitants. L'un des parages préférés des touristes est la très belle baie que les Romains appelaient «Portus Magnus». Aux alentours, on peut voir les catacombes ou la chapelle souterraine de Sainte Agnès, déclarées Monument National, et la grotte «Ses Fontanelles» où l'on peut admirer de belles peintures rupestres.

Located on the western part of Ibiza, 16 km (10 m) from the capital and in front of Conejera island. The town has 1 500 inhabitants. Its beautiful bay, called «Portus Magnus» by the Romans, is one of the favorite tourism places. Near the town is the Santa Inés catacomb or subterranean chapel, declared a National Monument, and the «Ses Fontanelles» cave, where interesting rupestrine paintings can be admired.

Liegt im Waesten von Ibiza, 16 Kilometer von der Hauptsdt entfernt und gegenüber der In-

sel Conejera. Die Stadt hat 1 500 Einwohner. Die schöne Bucht, welche die Romer «Portus Magnus» nannten, ist einer der bevorzugten Orte für den Fremdenverkehr. In der Nähe der Stadt befindet sich die Katakombe oder unterirdische Kapelle Sta. Inés, ein National denkmal, und die Höhle «Ses Fontanelles», in der man interessante prähostorische Male reien bewundern kann.

Santa Eulalia del Río

A 15 km de la capital de la isla, mirando al Levante, al pie del «Puig de Missa» —sobre el que se destaca la blanca silueta de su antigua iglesia-fortaleza— y a la izquierda del único río balear, se extiende el núcleo urbano de la villa, con unos 1 500 habitantes. En la iglesia de Nuestra Señora de Jesús se halla la pieza pictórica más valiosa de la isla: un retablo gótico de fines del siglo XV o comienzos del XVI, producto del taller valenciano de Rodrigo de Osona.

A 15 km du chef-lieu de l'île, tournée vers l'est, aux pied du «Puig de Missa», se découpe la silhouette blanche de la vieille église forteresse. A gauche de l'unique rivière baléare, s'étend une petite concentration urbaine avec 1 500 habitants. Dans l'église de Notre-Dame de Jésus, on trouve la pièce de plus grande valeur de l'île: il s'agit d'un retable gothique de la fin du XV ou début du XVIᵉ siècle d'un atelier de Valencia, de Rodrigo de Osona.

15 km (± 10 m.) from the island's capital looking East, at the foot of the «Puig de Missa» —on which is prominent the white silhouette of the old church-fortress— and to the left of the only Balearic river, is the urban nucleus, with about 1 500 inhabitants. The church of Our Lady of Jesus holds the pictorical piece of most importance in the island: a Gothic retable of the end of the XVth century and beginning of the XVIth, a product of the Valencian atelier of Rodrigo de Osona.

15 Kilometer von der Inselhauptstadt in östlicher Richtung entfernt, am Fuss des «Puig de Missa» gelegen, von welchem sich die weisse Silhouette der alten, befestigten Kirche abhebt, und auf der linken Seite des einzigen balearischen Flusses, breitet sich das Stadtzentrum der Ortes mit 1 500 Einwohnern aus. In der Kirche Nuestra Señora de Jesús befindet sich das malerisch wertvollste Stück der Insel: ein gotisches Altarbild vom Ende des XV. oder Anfang des XVI. Jahrhunderts, aus der werkstatt des Valencianers Rodrigo de Osona.

San José

Su centro urbano, de unos 500 habitantes, se halla en el interior, a 15 km de la capital, pero es el Municipio con más dilatado litoral, en continua sucesión de acantilados y playas. Custodio de las más puras esencias del folklore ibicenco. El islote del «Vedrá» (382 m), la «Atalayassa», pico culminante de la isla (475 m); la «Coba Santa» y las salinas son lugares del máximo interés turístico.

Ce centre urbain, d'environ 500 habitants, se trouve à l'intérieur, à 15 km du chef-lieu mais il s'agit de la commune la plus étendue du littoral avec une succession interminable de plages et de falaises. On y trouve les plus pures essences du folklore d'Ibiza. La petite île du «Vedrá» (582 m), la «Atalayassa», point culminant de l'île (475 m); la «Coba Santa» et les salines présentent un très vif intérêt touristique.

Its urban center, of about 500 inhabitants, is in the interior, 15 km (± 10 m) from the capital, but it is the Municipality with the largest sea-coast, in a continued succession of cliffs and beaches. It has the purest essences of Ibiza's folklore. The «Vedrá» islet (382 meters or 1253 ft), «Atalayassa», the highest peak in the island (475 m or 1558 ft); «Coba Santa» and the salt beds are places of maximum tourist interest.

Die Ortsmitte mit etwa 500 Einwohnern liegt im Landesinnern, 15 Kilometer von der Hauptstadt entfernt, es ist aber die Gemeinde mit dem längsten Küstenstreifen, wo Felsen küsten und Strände ständig abwechseln. Hier ist die Volkskunst Ibizas noch unberührt. Die kleine Insel «Vedrá» (382 Meter), «Atalayassa», höchster Gipfel der Insel (475 Meter), «Coba Santa» und die Salinen sind Orte von grossem touristischem Interesse.

San Juan Bautista

Situado al norte de la isla y a 22 km de su capital. Sus habitantes están muy diseminados en fincas de laboreo por todo el municipio. En la cueva de «Es Cuieram» se descubrió en 1907 un templo cartaginés dedicado a la diosa «Tanit». La única inscripción púnica hallada en España procede de esa demarcación. Digno de visitarse es el poblado-fortaleza de Balafi. Bellísimas calas de fina arena se encuentran en su litoral.

Situé ou nord de l'île et à 22 km du chef-lieu. Les habitants sont disséminés dans des propriétés agricoles sur toute la commune Dans la grotte de «Es Cuieram», on découvrit en 1907 un temple carthaginois dédié à la déesse «Tanit». L'unique inscription punique trouvée en Espagne provient de cette région. Il ne faut pas manquer de visiter le village fortifié de Balafi. Sur son littoral il y a de très belles criques de sable fin.

Located on the north of the island, 22 km (13,2 m) from the capital. Its inhabitants are spread in farms all over the Municipality. In «Es Cuieram» cave was discovered in 1907 a Carthagenian temple dedicated to goddess «Tanit». The only Punic inscription found in Spain comes from this locality. Worthy of visiting is the townshipfortress of Balafi. The sea coast has beautiful coves with very fine sand.

Liegt im Norden der Insel, 22 Kilometer von der Hauptstadt entfernt. Die Einwohner wohnen sehr zerstreut in Bauernhöfen, welche vereinzelt in der ganzen Gemeinde liegen. In der Höhle «Es Cuieram» wurde 1907 ein der Göttin «Tanit» gewidmeter karthagischer Tempel, entdeckt. Die einzige in Spanien gefundene punische Inschrift stammt aus dieser Gegend. Der befestigte Ort Balafi ist einen Besuch wert, wunderschöne Buchten mit feinem Sand liegen an seiner Küste.

FORMENTERA

San Francisco Javier

Capital de la isla. Blanco caserío, rodeando una iglesia fortificada, de una armonía y una simplicidad encantadoras. Bellísima playa de Cala Sabina. Se efectúan excursiones hacia el Oeste, la parte más salvaje de la isla, un gran valle que desemboca en la playa de Cala Sahona, dominada por el promontorio del Cabo Punta Rosa.

Chef-lieu de l'île. Agglomération blanche autour d'une église fortifiée dotée d'une grande harmonie et d'une simplicité charmante. Très belle plage de Cala Sabina. On fait des excursions vers l'ouest, la région la plus sauvage de l'île; une grande vallée qui débouche sur la plage de Cala Sahona est dominée par le promontoire du Cap Punta Rosa.

Capital of the island. White settlements, surounding a fortified church, with charming harmony and simplicity. Very beautiful beach in Cala Sabina. Tours are taken to the West, the wildest part of the island, a large valley ending at the Cala Sahona beach, dominated by the Cabo Punta Rosa promontory.

Hauptstadt der Insel. Es ist ein kleines, weisses Dorf mit einer befestigten Kirche, von einer entzückenden Harmonie und Einfachheit. Es gibt einen herrlichen Strand Cala Sabina. Es werden Ausflüge zum Westen der Insel durchgeführt. Dies ist der unberührteste Teil der Insel, ein grosses Teil, welches in den Strand Cala Sahona ausläuft, der von der Anhöhe des Caps Punta Rosa beherrscht wird.

La Sabina

Único puerto de la isla, con su docena de casas blancas y sus pequeños silos de sal.

Seul port de l'île, avec une douzaine de maisons blanches et de petits silos de sel.

Only port in the island, with a dozen white houses and its small salt silos.

Das ist der einzige Hafen der Insel mit einem Duzend weisser Häuser und kleinen Salzsilos.

San Fernando

Bosque de pinos y sabinas. Playa de Es Pujols. Hacia el sur, las vastas riberas que conducen a la playa Mitjorn. Hacia el Este, la belleza del puerto natural Es Caló.

Foret de pins et de sabines. Plage d'Es Pujols. En allant vers le sud, les grans rivages qui mènent à la plage Mitjorn. Vers l'est, le très beau port naturel Es Caló.

Pines and sabines forest. Es Pujols beach. To the South, the wide shores leading to Mitjorn beach. To the East, the beauty of the Es Caló natural port.

Pinienwald. Strand Es Pujols, Südlich die breiten Ufer, welche zum Strand Mitjorn führen, östlich Die Schönheit des Naturhafens Es Caló.

Nuestra Señora del Pilar

Excursión a La Mola, 192 m de altitud, donde se encuentra el faro.

Excursion à La Mola, 192 m d'altitude, où se trouve le phare.

Tour to La Mola, 192 m (approx. 630 ft.), where the lighthouse is located.

Ausflug nach La Mola, mit einer Höhe von 192 Metern und dem Leuchtturm.

INDICE

PUBLICACIONES EVEREST SOBRE LAS ISLAS BALEARES

GUIAS ARTISTICO-TURISTICAS
— IBIZA Y FORMENTERA, por Francisco Verdera
  Ediciones en Español, Francés, Inglés y Alemán.
— MALLORCA, por A. y L. Casasnovas
  Ediciones en Español, Francés, Inglés y Alemán.
— MENORCA, por A. y L. Casasnovas
  Ediciones en Español e Inglés.

COLECCION EVERTUR
— MALLORCA, por Juan Bonet
  Ediciones en Español, Francés, Inglés y Alemán.
— GUIA DICCIONARIO PARA EL TURISTA DE HABLA FRANCESA
— GUIA DICCIONARIO PARA EL TURISTA DE HABLA INGLESA

COLECCION HISPANICA
— IBIZA, por Carlos J. Taranilla
  Ediciones en Español, Francés, Inglés y Alemán.
— MALLORCA, por Carlos J. Taranilla
Ediciones en Español, Francés, Inglés y Alemán.

COLECCION IBERICA

— ASI ME GUSTA MALLORCA
Edición en Español, Francés, Inglés y Alemán.

— CUEVAS DE MALLORCA, por Pedro Santamarta
Ediciones en Español, Francés, Inglés y Alemán.

— MENORCA EN COLOR
Edición en Español, Francés, Inglés y Alemán.

CLUB EVEREST

— ESPAÑA TURISTICA

MAPAS TURISTICOS DE ESPAÑA

— MALLORCA

— MENORCA

— IBIZA Y FORMENTERA

MAPAS DE CARRETERAS

— ESPAÑA Y PORTUGAL, escala 1 : 500 000

— ESPAÑA Y PORTUGAL, escala 1 : 1 100 000

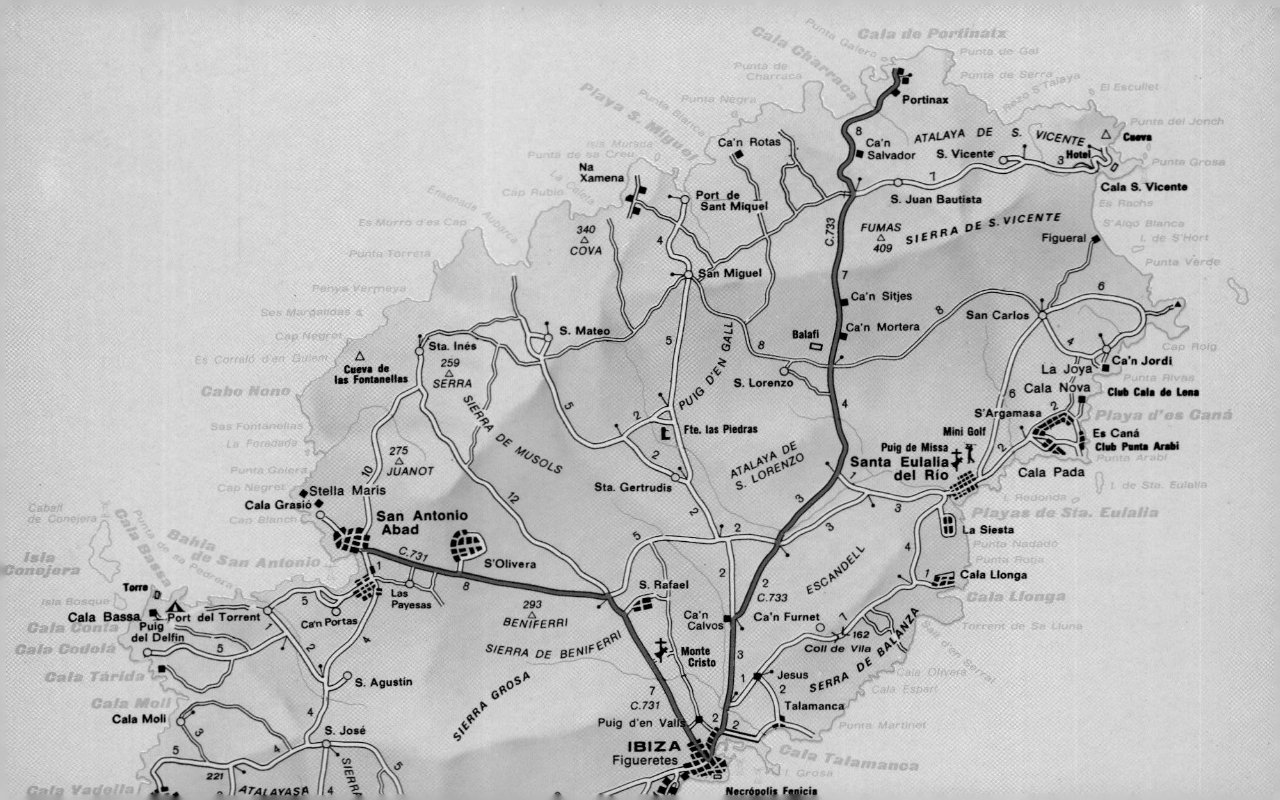

Cala de Portinatx
Cala Charraca
Portinax
Ca'n Salvador
ATALAYA DE S. VICENTE
S. Vicente
Cueva
Hotel
Cala S. Vicente
S. Juan Bautista
FUMAS
409
SIERRA DE S. VICENTE
Figueral
C.733
Playa S. Miguel
Ca'n Rotas
Na Xamena
Port de Sant Miquel
340
COVA
San Miguel
Ca'n Sitjes
Ca'n Mortera
Balafi
San Carlos
Ca'n Jordi
La Joya
Cala Nova
Club Cala de Lena
Playa d'es Caná
S'Argamasa
Mini Golf
Es Caná
Club Punta Arabi
Puig de Missa
Santa Eulalia del Río
Cala Pada
Playas de Sta. Eulalia
La Siesta
Cala Llonga
S. Mateo
Sta. Inés
259
SERRA
Cueva de las Fontanellas
Cabo Nono
PUIG D'EN GALL
S. Lorenzo
Fte. las Piedras
ATALAYA DE S. LORENZO
SIERRA DE MUSOLS
275
JUANOT
Stella Maris
Cala Grasió
San Antonio Abad
Sta. Gertrudis
ESCANDELL
Isla Conejera
Bahia de San Antonio
C.731
S'Olivera
Las Payesas
S. Rafael
Ca'n Calvos
Ca'n Furnet
Coll de Vila
162
Torre
Cala Bassa
Port del Torrent
Puig del Delfin
Ca'n Portas
293
BENIFERRI
SIERRA DE BENIFERRI
Monte Cristo
Jesus
SERRA DE BALANZA
Cala Conta
Cala Codolá
Cala Tárida
S. Agustín
SIERRA GROSA
Talamanca
Cala Moli
S. José
Puig d'en Valls
IBIZA
Figueretes
Cala Talamanca
Necrópolis Fenicia
Cala Vadella
221
ATALAYASA